Glencoe McGraw-Hill

Math Connects
Course 1

Chapter 7
Resource Masters

Consumable Workbooks Many of the worksheets contained in the Chapter Resource Masters are available as consumable workbooks in both English and Spanish.

	MHID	ISBN
Study Guide and Intervention Workbook	0-07-881032-9	978-0-07-881032-9
Skills Practice Workbook	0-07-881031-0	978-0-07-881031-2
Practice Workbook	0-07-881034-5	978-0-07-881034-3
Word Problem Practice Workbook	0-07-881033-7	978-0-07-881033-6

Spanish Versions

	MHID	ISBN
Study Guide and Intervention Workbook	0-07-881036-1	978-0-07-881036-7
Skills Practice Workbook	0-07-881035-3	978-0-07-881035-0
Practice Workbook	0-07-881038-8	978-0-07-881038-1
Word Problem Practice Workbook	0-07-881037-x	978-0-07-881037-4

Answers for Workbooks The answers for Chapter 7 of these workbooks can be found in the back of this Chapter Resource Masters booklet.

StudentWorks Plus™ This CD-ROM includes the entire Student Edition test along with the English workbooks listed above.

TeacherWorks Plus™ All of the materials found in this booklet are included for viewing, printing, and editing in this CD-ROM.

Spanish Assessment Masters (MHID: 0-07-881039-6, ISBN: 978-0-07-881039-8) These masters contain a Spanish version of Chapter 7 Test Form 2A and Form 2C.

 Glencoe

The McGraw·Hill Companies

Send all inquiries to:
Glencoe/McGraw-Hill
8787 Orion Place
Columbus, OH 43240

ISBN: 978-0-07-881025-1
MHID: 0-07-881025-6

Math Connects, Course 1

Printed in the United States of America.
1 2 3 4 5 6 7 8 9 10 047 16 15 14 13 12 11 10 09 08 07

CONTENTS

Teacher's Guide to Using the
Chapter 7 Resource Masters

The *Chapter 7 Resource Masters* includes the core materials needed for Chapter 7. These materials include worksheets, extensions, and assessment options. The answers for these pages appear at the back of this booklet.

All of the materials found in this booklet are included for viewing and printing on the *TeacherWorks Plus™* CD-ROM.

Chapter Resources

Student-Built Glossary (pages 1–2) These masters are a student study tool that presents up to twenty of the key vocabulary terms from the chapter. Students are to record definitions and/or examples for each term. You may suggest that students highlight or star the terms with which they are not familiar. Give this to students before beginning Lesson 7-1. Encourage them to add these pages to their mathematics study notebooks. Remind them to complete the appropriate words as they study each lesson.

Family Letter and Family Activity (pages 3–6) The letter informs your students' families of the mathematics they will be learning in this chapter. The family activity helps them to practice problems that are similar to those on the state test. A full solution for each problem is included. Spanish versions of these pages are also included. Give these to students to take home before beginning the chapter.

Anticipation Guide (pages 7–8) This master, presented in both English and Spanish, is a survey used before beginning the chapter to pinpoint what students may or may not know about the concepts in the chapter. Students will revisit this survey after they complete the chapter to see if their perceptions have changed.

Lesson Resources

Lesson Reading Guide Get Ready for the Lesson reiterates the questions from the beginning of the Student Edition lesson. Read the Lesson asks students to interpret the context of and relationships among terms in the lesson. Finally, Remember What You Learned asks students to summarize what they have learned using various representation techniques. Use as a study tool for note taking or as an informal reading assignment. It is also a helpful tool for ELL (English Language Learners).

Study Guide and Intervention This master provides vocabulary, key concepts, additional worked-out examples and Check Your Progress exercises to use as a reteaching activity. It can also be used in conjunction with the Student Edition as an instructional tool for students who have been absent.

Skills Practice This master focuses more on the computational nature of the lesson. Use as an additional practice option or as homework for second-day teaching of the lesson.

Practice This master closely follows the types of problems found in the Exercises section of the Student Edition and includes word problems. Use as an additional practice option or as homework for second-day teaching of the lesson.

Word Problem Practice This master includes additional practice in solving word problems that apply the concepts of the lesson. Use as an additional practice or as homework for second-day teaching of the lesson.

Enrichment These activities may extend the concepts of the lesson, offer a historical or multicultural look at the concepts, or widen students' perspectives on the mathematics they are learning. They are written for use with all levels of students.

Graphing Calculator, Scientific Calculator, or Spreadsheet Activities These activities present ways in which technology can be used with the concepts in some lessons of this chapter. Use as an alternative approach to some concepts or as an integral part of your lesson presentation.

Assessment Options

The assessment masters in the *Chapter 7 Resource Masters* offer a wide range of assessment tools for formative (monitoring) assessment and summative (final) assessment.

Student Recording Sheet This master corresponds with the Test Practice at the end of the chapter.

Extended-Response Rubric This master provides information for teachers and students on how to assess performance on open-ended questions.

Quizzes Four free-response quizzes offer assessment at appropriate intervals in the chapter.

Mid-Chapter Test This 1-page test provides an option to assess the first half of the chapter. It parallels the timing of the Mid-Chapter Quiz in the Student Edition and includes both multiple-choice and free-response questions.

Vocabulary Test This test is suitable for all students. It includes a list of vocabulary words and 10 questions to assess students' knowledge of those words. This can also be used in conjunction with one of the leveled chapter tests.

Leveled Chapter Tests

- *Form 1* contains multiple-choice questions and is intended for use with below grade level students.

- *Forms 2A and 2B* contain multiple-choice questions aimed at on grade level students. These tests are similar in format to offer comparable testing situations.

- *Forms 2C and 2D* contain free-response questions aimed at on grade level students. These tests are similar in format to offer comparable testing situations.

- *Form 3* is a free-response test for use with above grade level students.

All of the above mentioned tests include a free-response Bonus question.

Extended-Response Test Performance assessment tasks are suitable for all students. Samples answers and a scoring rubric are included for evaluation.

Standardized Test Practice These three pages are cumulative in nature. It includes two parts: multiple-choice questions with bubble-in answer format and short-answer free-response questions.

Answers

- The answers for the Anticipation Guide and Lesson Resources are provided as reduced pages with answers appearing in red.

- Full-size answer keys are provided for the assessment masters.

7 Student-Built Glossary

This is an alphabetical list of new vocabulary terms you will learn in Chapter 7. As you study the chapter, complete each term's definition or description. Remember to add the page number where you found the term. Add this page to your math study notebook to review vocabulary at the end of the chapter.

Vocabulary Term	Found on Page	Definition/Description/Example
complementary events		
circle graph		
experimental probability		
Fundamental Counting Principle		
outcomes		
percent		
population		
probability		
random		

7 Student-Built Glossary (continued)

Vocabulary Term	Found on Page	Definition/Description/Example
sample		
sample space		
simple event		
survey [sir-vay]		
theoretical probability [thee-uh-REHT-uh-kuhl] [prah-buh-BILL-uh-tee]		
tree diagram		

7 **Family Letter**

Dear Parent or Guardian:

We can use probability to help us determine how often or how likely something is to occur. For example, we know that when we toss a coin, the probability that it will land faceup is $\frac{1}{2}$ or 50% of the time. Knowing percent and probability can help us make more informed decisions.

In **Chapter 7, Percent and Probability**, your child will learn how decimals, fractions, and percents relate. In addition, your child will learn how to interpret and apply the probability of an event. Finally, your child will learn to estimate with percents. In the study of this chapter, your child will complete a variety of daily classroom assignments and activities and possibly produce a chapter project.

By signing this letter and returning it with your child, you agree to encourage your child by getting involved. Enclosed is an activity you can do with your child that practices how the math we will be learning in Chapter 7 might be tested. You may also wish to log on to **glencoe.com** for self-check quizzes and other study help. If you have any questions or comments, feel free to contact me at school.

Sincerely,

Signature of Parent or Guardian _____ Date _____

7 Family Activity

State Test Practice

Fold the page along the dashed line. Work each problem on another piece of paper. Then unfold the page to check your work.

1. Devon reaches into a bag containing six yellow tiles and 8 green tiles. What is the probability that he will pull out a green tile?

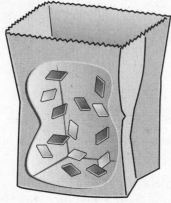

    A $\frac{8}{16}$

    B $\frac{8}{14}$

    C $\frac{6}{14}$

    D $\frac{6}{8}$

2. A survey was conducted at a local middle school. One hundred students were asked to name their favorite color. Here are the results.

Favorite Colors at Blues Middle School

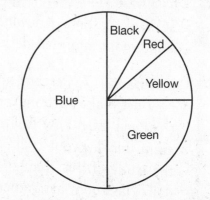

About what percentage of the students said green is their favorite color?

    A 20%

    B 25%

    C 33%

    D 50%

Fold here.

- -

Solution

1. *Hint: The probability of a specific event occurring is the number of times it would be possible for the specific event to occur over the total number of events.*

   The bag contains 8 green tiles and 6 yellow tiles, or a total of 14 tiles. The probability of choosing a green one is the number of green tiles (8) over the total number of tiles (14), which can be represented as $\frac{8}{14}$.

   The answer is **B.**

Solution

2. Green represents one-fourth of the circle shown in the graph, which means that $\frac{1}{4}$ of the students chose green as their favorite color. One-fourth, or one quarter of the circle is 25%. You can also calculate the percentage from the fraction by either dividing the numerator by the denominator and multiplying by 100% or setting up a ratio for the percentage, in this case:

$$\frac{1}{4} = \frac{?}{100}$$

   The answer is **B.**

7 Carta a la familia

Estimado padre o apoderado:

Usamos las probabilidades para ayudarnos a determinar la frecuencia o posibilidad de que algo ocurra. Por ejemplo, sabemos que al lanzar una moneda, la probabilidad de que caiga en cara es $\frac{1}{2}$ ó el 50% de las veces. Saber de porcentajes y probabilidades nos ayuda a tomar decisiones más informadas.

En el **Capítulo 7, Porcentajes y probabilidad**, su hijo(a) aprenderá la relación entre decimales, fracciones y porcentajes. Además, su hijo(a) aprenderá a interpretar y a aplicar la probabilidad de un evento. Finalmente, su hijo(a) aprenderá a estimar con porcentajes. En el estudio de este capítulo, su hijo(a) completará una variedad de tareas y actividades diarias y es posible que trabaje en un proyecto del capítulo.

Al firmar esta carta y devolverla con su hijo(a), usted se compromete a ayudarlo(a) a participar en su aprendizaje. Junto con esta carta, va incluida una actividad que puede realizar con él(ella) y la cual practica lo que podrían encontrar en las pruebas de los conceptos matemáticos que aprenderán en el Capítulo 7. Además, visiten **glencoe.com** para ver autocontroles y otras ayudas para el estudio. Si tiene cualquier pregunta o comentario, por favor contácteme en la escuela.

Cordialmente,

Firma del padre o apoderado _____ Fecha _____

7 Actividad en familia

Práctica para la prueba estatal

Doblen la página a lo largo de las líneas punteadas. Resuelvan cada problema en otra hoja de papel. Luego, desdoblen la página y revisen las respuestas.

1. Devon mete la mano en una bolsa que contiene seis fichas amarillas y ocho verdes. ¿Cuál es la probabilidad de que saque una verde?

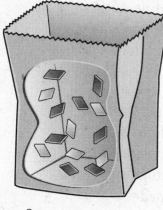

   A $\frac{8}{16}$

   B $\frac{8}{14}$

   C $\frac{6}{14}$

   D $\frac{6}{8}$

2. Se condujo un sondeo en una escuela intermedia. Se les pidió a cien alumnos que nombraran su color favorito. He aquí los resultados.

Colores favoritos en la escuela intermedia Blues

¿Alrededor de qué porcentaje de alumnos dijo que su color favorito era el verde?

   A 20%

   B 25%

   C 33%

   D 50%

Doblen aquí.

Solución

1. *Ayuda: La probabilidad de que ocurra un evento específico es el número de veces posibles que dicho evento ocurriera sobre el número total de eventos*

   La bolsa contiene 8 fichas verdes y 6 amarillas o un total de 14 fichas. La probabilidad de elegir una verde es el número de fichas verdes (8) sobre el número total de fichas (14), lo que puede representarse como $\frac{8}{14}$.

Solución

2. El verde representa un cuarto del círculo que muestra la gráfica, lo cual significa que $\frac{1}{4}$ de los alumnos escogió el verde como su color favorito. Una cuarta parte o un cuarto del círculo es 25%. También puedes calcular el porcentaje de la fracción, al dividir el numerador entre el denominador y multiplicar por 100% o fijar una razón para el porcentaje, en este caso:

$$\frac{1}{4} = \frac{?}{100}$$

La respuesta es **B**.

La respuesta es **B**.

7 Anticipation Guide

Percent and Probability

STEP 1 Before you begin Chapter 7

- Read each statement.

- Decide whether you Agree (A) or Disagree (D) with the statement.

- Write A or D in the first column OR if you are not sure whether you agree or disagree, write NS (Not Sure).

STEP 1 A, D, or NS	Statement	STEP 2 A or D
	1. Percent means *hundredths*.	
	2. To write a fraction as a percent, multiply the fraction by $\frac{1}{100}$.	
	3. In a circle graph the percents add up to 360%.	
	4. By comparing the size of the sections in a circle graph you can compare the data represented by those sections.	
	5. Moving the decimal point in a number two places to the left is the same as dividing that number by 100.	
	6. To write a decimal as a percent, first write the decimal as a fraction with a denominator of 100.	
	7. The probability that an event will occur is always a number from 0 to 100.	
	8. A tree diagram can be used to find the number of possible outcomes of an event.	
	9. To have an accurate survey of a group of people, all people in the group must be surveyed.	
	10. 85 is a good estimate of 48% of 150.	

STEP 2 After you complete Chapter 7

- Reread each statement and complete the last column by entering an A (Agree) or a D (Disagree).

- Did any of your opinions about the statements change from the first column?

- For those statements that you mark with a D, use a separate sheet of paper to explain why you disagree. Use examples, if possible.

7 Ejercicios preparatorios
Porcentaje y probabilidad

PASO 1 *Antes de comenzar el Capítulo 7*

- Lee cada enunciado.

- Decide si estás de acuerdo (A) o en desacuerdo (D) con el enunciado.

- Escribe A o D en la primera columna O si no estás seguro(a) de la respuesta, escribe NS (No estoy seguro(a)).

PASO 1 A, D o NS	Enunciado	PASO 2 A o D
	1. Porcentaje significa *centésimas*.	
	2. Para escribir una fracción como porcentaje, multiplica la fracción por $\frac{1}{100}$.	
	3. En una gráfica circular, los porcentajes suman hasta 360%.	
	4. Al comparar el tamaño de los sectores en una gráfica circular, puedes comparar la información representada por estas secciones.	
	5. Mover el punto decimal de un número dos lugares a la izquierda es lo mismo que dividir dicho número entre 100.	
	6. Para escribir un decimal como porcentaje, primero escribe el decimal como una fracción con denominador de 100.	
	7. La probabilidad de que un evento ocurra siempre es un número de 0 a 100.	
	8. Un diagrama de árbol puede utilizarse para encontrar el número de posibles resultados de un evento.	
	9. Para obtener una encuesta precisa de un grupo de personas, se debe encuestar a todas las personas en el grupo.	
	10. Un buen estimado del 48% de 150 es 85.	

PASO 2 *Después de completar el Capítulo 7*

- Vuelve a leer cada enunciado y completa la última columna con una A o una D.

- ¿Cambió cualquiera de tus opiniones sobre los enunciados de la primera columna?

- En una hoja de papel aparte, escribe un ejemplo de por qué estás en desacuerdo con los enunciados que marcaste con una D.

7-1 Lesson Reading Guide

Percents and Fractions

Get Ready for the Lesson

Read the introduction at the top of page 365 in your textbook. Write your answers below.

1. What ratio compares the number of students who prefer grape fruit bars to the total number of students?

2. Draw a decimal model to represent this ratio.

3. What fraction represents this ratio?

Read the Lesson

4. Write the two steps to use to write a percent as a fraction.

5. Look at the graph at the top of page 365. What is the sum of the number of students? Look at Example 3. Based on the information given, what percentage of cell phone owners said that they do not use the text messaging feature? How do you know?

6. Look at Example 2 on page 366. Why is 125% written as a mixed number?

Remember What You Learned

7. Write a fraction as a percent using the steps shown in Examples 4 and 5 on pages 366 and 367. Choose any fraction you like different from those in the Examples.

Step	Equation(s)
Set up a proportion.	
Write the cross products.	
Multiply.	
Divide.	
Conclusion.	So, _____ is equivalent to _____.

7-1 Study Guide and Intervention

Percents and Fractions

To write a percent as a fraction, write it as a fraction with a denominator of 100. Then simplify.

Example 1 Write 15% as a fraction in simplest form.

15% means *15 out of 100*.

$$15\% = \frac{15}{100}$$ Definition of percent.

$$= \frac{\overset{3}{\cancel{15}}}{\underset{20}{\cancel{100}}} \text{ or } \frac{3}{20}$$ Simplify. Divide the numerator and denominator by the GCF, 5.

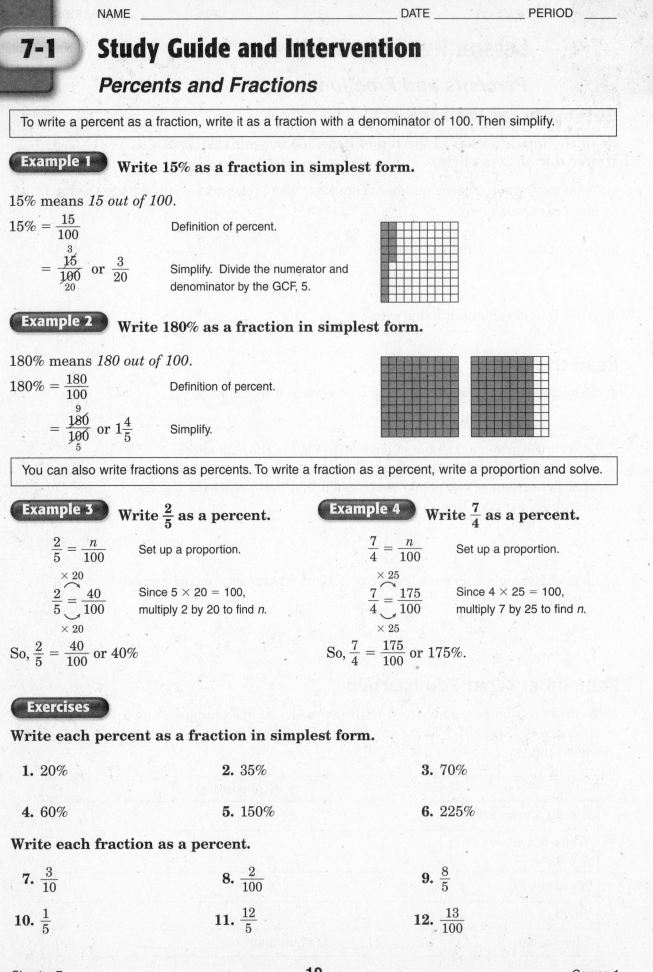

Example 2 Write 180% as a fraction in simplest form.

180% means *180 out of 100*.

$$180\% = \frac{180}{100}$$ Definition of percent.

$$= \frac{\overset{9}{\cancel{180}}}{\underset{5}{\cancel{100}}} \text{ or } 1\frac{4}{5}$$ Simplify.

You can also write fractions as percents. To write a fraction as a percent, write a proportion and solve.

Example 3 Write $\frac{2}{5}$ as a percent.

$$\frac{2}{5} = \frac{n}{100}$$ Set up a proportion.

$$\frac{2}{5} \overset{\times 20}{\underset{\times 20}{=}} \frac{40}{100}$$ Since 5 × 20 = 100, multiply 2 by 20 to find *n*.

So, $\frac{2}{5} = \frac{40}{100}$ or 40%

Example 4 Write $\frac{7}{4}$ as a percent.

$$\frac{7}{4} = \frac{n}{100}$$ Set up a proportion.

$$\frac{7}{4} \overset{\times 25}{\underset{\times 25}{=}} \frac{175}{100}$$ Since 4 × 25 = 100, multiply 7 by 25 to find *n*.

So, $\frac{7}{4} = \frac{175}{100}$ or 175%.

Exercises

Write each percent as a fraction in simplest form.

1. 20%   **2.** 35%   **3.** 70%

4. 60%   **5.** 150%   **6.** 225%

Write each fraction as a percent.

7. $\frac{3}{10}$ **8.** $\frac{2}{100}$ **9.** $\frac{8}{5}$

10. $\frac{1}{5}$ **11.** $\frac{12}{5}$ **12.** $\frac{13}{100}$

7-1 Skills Practice

Percents and Fractions

Write each percent as a fraction in simplest form.

1. 40%

2. 30%

3. 55%

4. 75%

5. 140%

6. 175%

7. 24%

8. 68%

9. 44%

10. 92%

11. 110%

12. 155%

13. 18%

14. 74%

15. 43%

Write each fraction as a percent.

16. $\frac{4}{5}$

17. $\frac{3}{20}$

18. $\frac{7}{10}$

19. $\frac{3}{5}$

20. $\frac{3}{2}$

21. $\frac{5}{4}$

22. $\frac{6}{5}$

23. $\frac{9}{20}$

24. $\frac{13}{20}$

25. $\frac{17}{20}$

26. $\frac{9}{5}$

27. $\frac{11}{10}$

28. $\frac{19}{20}$

29. $\frac{13}{10}$

30. $\frac{21}{100}$

Lesson 7-1

7-1 **Practice**

Percents and Fractions

Write each percent as a fraction in simplest form.

1. 60%   **2.** 18%   **3.** 4%

4. 35%   **5.** 10%   **6.** 1%

7. 175%   **8.** 258%   **9.** 325%

10. ENERGY The United States uses 24% of the world's supply of energy. What fraction of the world's energy is this?

Write each fraction as a percent.

11. $\frac{6}{10}$ **12.** $\frac{2}{5}$ **13.** $\frac{9}{5}$

14. $\frac{6}{4}$ **15.** $\frac{7}{100}$ **16.** $\frac{4}{100}$

Write a percent to represent the shaded portion of each model.

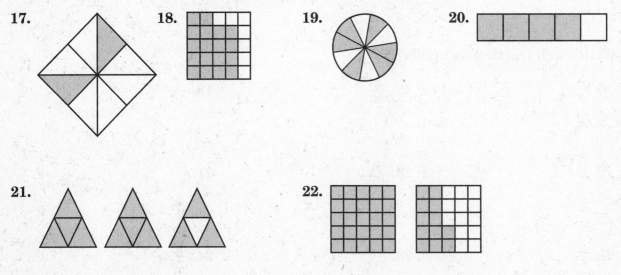

17.   **18.**   **19.**   **20.**

21.   **22.**

23. ANALYZE TABLES The table shows what fraction of a vegetable garden contains each kind of vegetable. What percent of the garden contains other kinds of vegetables?

Plant	Beans	Corn	Tomatoes	Other
Fraction	$\frac{1}{5}$	$\frac{1}{2}$	$\frac{1}{4}$	■

7-1 Word Problem Practice

Percents and Fractions

Lesson 7-1

1. **TOYS** The Titanic Toy Company has a 4% return rate on its products. Write this percent as a fraction in simplest form.

2. **MUSIC** There are 4 trombones out of 25 instruments in the Landers town band. What percent of the instruments are trombones?

3. **SHOPPING** Alicia's favorite clothing store is having a 30% off sale. What fraction represents the 30% off sale?

4. **FOOD** At Ben's Burger Palace, 45% of the customers order large soft drinks. What fraction of the customers order large soft drinks?

5. **BASKETBALL** In a recent NBA season, Shaquille O'Neal of the Los Angeles Lakers made 60% of his field goals. What fraction of his field goals did Shaquille make?

6. **SCHOOL** In Janie's class, 7 out of 25 students have blue eyes. What percent of the class has blue eyes?

7. **TESTS** Michael answered $\frac{17}{20}$ questions correctly on his test. What percent of the questions did Michael answer correctly?

8. **RESTAURANTS** On Saturday afternoon, $\frac{41}{50}$ telephone calls taken at The Overlook restaurant were for dinner reservations. What percent of the telephone calls were for dinner reservations?

7-1 Enrichment

It's On Sale!

Stores have sales to attract people to buy their merchandise or to sell off seasonal merchandise at the end of a season. They may advertise 20% off the regular price of an item or $\frac{1}{2}$ off the regular price. Sometimes, stores will offer an extra sale on top of the sale price.

Stores usually advertise the sale price as a percentage or a fraction off the original price. Savvy shoppers know how percentages and fractions compare to know which is a better deal.

Write a fraction representing how much off the regular price is the store offering.

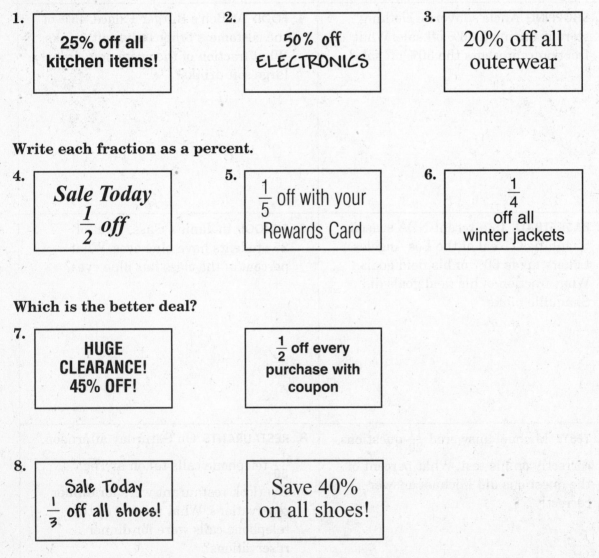

1.

**25% off all
kitchen items!**

2.

50% off
ELECTRONICS

3.

20% off all
outerwear

Write each fraction as a percent.

4.

Sale Today
$\frac{1}{2}$ *off*

5.

$\frac{1}{5}$ off with your
Rewards Card

6.

$\frac{1}{4}$
off all
winter jackets

Which is the better deal?

7.

**HUGE
CLEARANCE!
45% OFF!**

$\frac{1}{2}$ off every
purchase with
coupon

8.

Sale Today
$\frac{1}{3}$ off all shoes!

Save 40%
on all shoes!

7-2 Lesson Reading Guide

Circle Graphs

Get Ready for the Lesson

Complete the Mini Lab at the top of page 370 in your textbook. Write your answers below.

1. Make a bar graph of the data.

2. Which graph represents the data better, a circle graph or a bar graph? Explain.

Read the Lesson

3. A circle graph compares parts of a whole. How is a circle well suited for this kind of representation?

4. At the bottom of page 370, the text says that the percents add up to 100%. Why is this important?

Remember What You Learned

5. Find a circle graph in a newspaper or magazine. Explain to a classmate what the sections of the graph represent.

Lesson 7-2

7-2 Study Guide and Intervention

Circle Graphs

A **circle graph** is used to compare data that are parts of a whole. The pie-shaped sections show the groups. The percents add up to 100%.

Example 1 The table shows the time Mike spends studying each subject during homework time. Sketch a circle graph of the data.

Mike's Homework	
Subject	**Percent**
math	50%
social studies	15%
reading	25%
science	10%

- Write each percent as a fraction.

  $50\% = \frac{50}{100}$ or $\frac{1}{2}$ $15\% = \frac{15}{100}$ or $\frac{3}{20}$

  $25\% = \frac{25}{100}$ or $\frac{1}{4}$ $10\% = \frac{10}{100}$ or $\frac{1}{10}$

- Use a compass to draw a circle.

- Since $50\% = \frac{1}{2}$, shade and label $\frac{1}{2}$ of the circle for math.

  Since $25\% = \frac{1}{4}$, shade and label $\frac{1}{4}$ of the circle for reading.

  Split the remaining section so that one section is slightly larger than the other. Label the slightly larger section social studies for 15%, and the smaller one science for 10%.

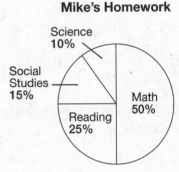

Mike's Homework

Example 2 In the circle graph to the right, how does the amount of time Mike spends studying math compare to the amount of time he studies reading?

The section representing math is twice the size of the section representing reading. So, Mike spends twice as much time studying math as reading.

Exercises

SURVEYS Use the table that shows the results of a favorite colors survey.

1. Sketch a circle graph of the data.

Favorite Color	
Color	**Percent**
blue	33%
red	25%
green	25%
purple	10%
yellow	7%

2. In your circle graph, which two sections represent the responses by the same amount of students?

3. In your circle graph, how does the number of students that chose blue compare to the number of students that chose purple?

7-2 Skills Practice

Circle Graphs

1. **VACATIONS** The table shows how families will spend their winter vacation. Sketch a circle graph of the data.

Winter Vacation	
Activity	**Percent**
visit family	33%
stay home	25%
shop	22%
ski	10%
beach	10%

2. **LAKES** The table shows how much of the total surface of the Great Lakes each lake takes up. Sketch a circle graph of the data.

Great Lakes	
Lake	**Percent**
Superior	34%
Huron	24%
Michigan	24%
Erie	10%
Ontario	8%

GEOGRAPHY For Exercises 3–6, use the graph below that shows how much of Earth's land that each continent represents.

3. Which continent has the greatest area?

4. Which two continents are the smallest?

5. How does the size of Europe compare to the size of Africa?

6. How much larger is Asia than Africa?

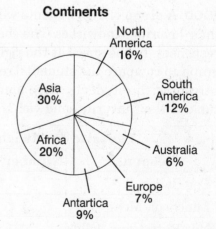

Continents

Lesson 7-2

7-2 Practice

Circle Graphs

1. **MUSIC** The table shows the percent of students in the school orchestra who played in each section. Sketch a circle graph to display the data.

Players in the Orchestra	
Section	Percent of Players
Brass	25%
Percussion	5%
Strings	45%
Woodwinds	25%

BLOOD For Exercises 2–5, use the graph that shows the percent of Americans having different blood types.

2. Which blood type is the least common among people of the United States?

3. About how much of the total U.S. population has Type O blood?

4. Which two sections of the graph represent about the same percent of people? Explain your reasoning.

Blood Types in the U.S. Population

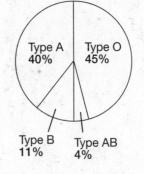

5. How does Type A compare to Type AB in number of people having these two types?

6. **FOOD** A group of 100 students were asked about their favorite sandwiches. The chart shows their responses. In the space at the right, sketch a circle graph to compare the students' responses. What percent of the students chose luncheon meat or tuna as their favorite sandwich?

Favorite Sandwich	
Response	Number of Students
Egg Salad	12
Luncheon Meat	51
Nut Butter and Jelly	24
Tuna	11
Other	2

18

7-2 **Word Problem Practice**

Circle Graphs

SPORTS For Exercises 1–3, use Graph A. For Exercises 4–6, use Graph B.

Graph A

Favorite Sports of Mr. Franco's Class

Baseball 49%
Hockey 10%
Football 21%
Basketball 20%

Graph B

Attendance at the Baseball Game

Age 46-60 14%
Age 61 and older 5%
Age 0-15 25%
Age 31-45 21%
Age 16-30 35%

1. Kwan surveyed Mr. Franco's class to find out the favorite sports of the class. Which sport was the favorite of the largest percent of students in the class? Which sport was the favorite of the smallest percent of students?

2. Which sports were the favorite of about the same number of students?

3. Which sport is the favorite of half as many students as basketball?

4. Mr. Jackson kept track of attendance at the baseball game for an advertising agency. The agency wants to target its advertising to the age group that has the highest percent in attendance. To which group should the agency target ads?

5. Which two age groups have about the same percent of people?

6. Mr. Jackson's daughter is in the age group with the second highest percent. In which age group is Mr. Jackson's daughter?

Lesson 7-2

7-2   Enrichment

A Circle Graph Mystery

The circle graph below was drawn to show the leading causes of fire in the
United States. However, all the labels except one have mysteriously disappeared.

**Use the clues below to decide what the labels
should be and where they belong. Then complete
the graph. (Remember: Each label must include a
word or phrase and a percent.)**

Causes of Fires

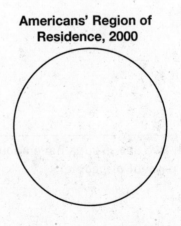

Clue 1	Most fires are caused by *heating equipment*.
Clue 2	Fires caused by *electrical wiring* and fires caused by *heating equipment* together make up 46% of all fires.
Clue 3	The percent of fires caused by *children playing* is 12% less than the percent of fires caused by *cooking*.
Clue 4	The percent of fires caused by *open flames* is equal to the percent of fires caused by *children playing*.
Clue 5	The percent of the fires caused by *cooking* and the percent of fires caused by *arson* are together just 1% less than the percent of fires caused by *heating equipment*.
Clue 6	The percent of the fires caused by *electrical wiring* is 15% greater than the percent caused by *children playing*.
Clue 7	Fires caused by *smoking* and fires caused by *arson* together make up 17% of all fires.
Clue 8	Fires that result from other causes are listed in a category called *other*.

Exercise

How well can you picture data? In the
space at the right, sketch a circle graph
to show the data below.

**Americans' Region of
Residence, 2000**

Americans' Region of Residence, 2000	
Northeast	19%
Midwest	23%
South	35%
West	23%

7-3 Lesson Reading Guide

Percents and Decimals

Get Ready for the Lesson

**Read the introduction at the top of page 377 in your textbook.
Write your answers below.**

1. What percent does the entire circle graph represent?

2. What fraction represents the section of the graph labeled math?

3. Write the fraction from Exercise 2 as a decimal.

Read the Lesson

Complete each of the following sentences.

4. To rewrite a fraction with a denominator of 100 as a decimal, move the
   decimal point of the numerator _____ places to the _____.

5. To rewrite a fraction with a denominator of _____ as a decimal, move
   the decimal point of the numerator 3 places to the left.

6. Look at Example 6 on page 378. Why do you multiply the numerator and
   denominator by 10?

Remember What You Learned

7. Look at Example 5 on page 378. Explain why you first write the decimal as
   a mixed number. Then explain what happens at the next step.

Lesson 7-3

7-3 Study Guide and Intervention

Percents and Decimals

To write a percent as a decimal, first rewrite the percent as a fraction with a denominator of 100. Then write the fraction as a decimal.

Example 1 Write 23% as a decimal.

$23\% = \dfrac{23}{100}$ Rewrite the percent as a fraction with a denominator of 100.

$= 0.23$ Write the fraction as a decimal.

Example 2 Write 127% as a decimal.

$127\% = \dfrac{127}{100}$ Rewrite the percent as a fraction with a denominator of 100.

$= 1.27$ Write the fraction as a decimal.

To write a decimal as a percent, first write the decimal as a fraction with a denominator of 100. Then write the fraction as a percent.

Example 3 Write 0.44 as a percent.

$0.44 = \dfrac{44}{100}$ Write the decimal as a fraction.

$= 44\%$ Write the fraction as a percent.

Example 4 Write 2.65 as a percent.

$2.65 = 2\dfrac{65}{100}$ Write 2 and 65 hundredths as a mixed number.

$= \dfrac{265}{100}$ Write the mixed number as an improper fraction.

$= 265\%$ Write the fraction as a percent.

Exercises

Write each percent as a decimal.

1. 39%   2. 57%   3. 82%

4. 135%   5. 112%   6. 0.4%

Write each decimal as a percent.

7. 0.86   8. 0.36   9. 0.65

10. 0.2   11. 1.48   12. 2.17

7-3 Skills Practice

Percents and Decimals

Write each percent as a decimal.

1. 5%

2. 8%

3. 37%

4. 12%

5. 29%

6. 54%

7. 48%

8. 79%

9. 0.1%

10. 0.6%

11. 0.2%

12. 0.5%

13. 123%

14. 102%

15. 135%

16. 310%

Write each decimal as a percent.

17. 0.3

18. 0.7

19. 0.19

20. 0.74

21. 0.66

22. 0.52

23. 0.21

24. 0.81

25. 0.13

26. 1.36

27. 5.28

28. 2.45

29. 1.94

30. 3.34

31. 4.26

32. 5.99

Lesson 7-3

7-3 Practice

Percents and Decimals

Express each percent as a decimal.

1. 29%   **2.** 63%   **3.** 4%   **4.** 9%

5. 148%   **6.** 106%   **7.** 10%   **8.** 32%

9. ENERGY The United States gets about 39% of its energy from petroleum. Write 39% as a decimal.

10. SCIENCE About 8% of the earth's crust is made up of aluminum. Write 8% as a decimal.

Express each decimal as a percent.

11. 0.45   **12.** 0.12   **13.** 1.68   **14.** 2.73

15. 0.2   **16.** 0.7   **17.** 0.95   **18.** 0.46

19. POPULATION In 2000, the number of people 65 years and older in Arizona was 0.13 of the total population. Write 0.13 as a percent.

20. GEOGRAPHY About 0.41 of Hawaii's total area is water. What percent is equivalent to 0.41?

Replace each ● with <, >, or = to make a true sentence.

21. 26% ● 0.3   **22.** 0.9 ● 9%   **23.** 4.7 ● 47%

24. ANALYZE TABLES A batting average is the ratio of hits to at bats. Batting averages are expressed as a decimal rounded to the nearest thousandth. Show two different ways of finding how much greater Derek Jeter's batting average was than Jason Giambi's batting average. Express as a percent.

New York Yankees, 2005 Batting Statistics	
Player	**Batting Average**
Jason Giambi	0.286
Derek Jeter	0.307
Hideki Matsui	0.297
Jorge Posada	0.257

Source: ESPN

7-3 Word Problem Practice

Percents and Decimals

---

1. **COMMUTING** According to the U.S. census, 76% of U.S. workers commute to work by driving alone. Write 76% as a decimal.

2. **BASEBALL** A player's batting average was 0.29 rounded to the nearest hundredth. Write 0.29 as a percent.

---

3. **ELECTIONS** In a recent U.S. midterm elections, 39% of eligible adults voted. What is 39% written as a decimal?

4. **BASKETBALL** In a recent season, Jason Kidd of the New Jersey Nets had a field goal average of 0.40 rounded to the nearest hundredth. What is 0.40 written as a percent?

---

5. **SPORTS** When asked to choose their favorite sport, 27% of U.S. adults who follow sports selected professional football. What decimal is equivalent to 27%?

6. **AGE** Lawrence is 18 years old and his brother Luther is 12 years old. This means that Lawrence is 1.5 times older than Luther. What percent is equivalent to 1.5?

---

7. **WATER** About 5% of the surface area of the U.S. is water. What decimal represents the amount of the U.S. surface area taken up by water?

8. **POPULATION** China accounts for 0.21 of the world's population. What percent of the world's population lives in China?

Lesson 7-3

7-3 Enrichment

Percent and Per Mill

A **percent** is a ratio that compares a number to 100.

$$\frac{83}{100} = 83 \text{ percent} = 83\% = 0.83$$

A ratio that compares a number to 1,000 is called a **per mill**. Just like percent, the ratio *per mill* has a special symbol, ‰.

$$\frac{83}{1,000} = 83 \text{ per mill} = 83‰ = 0.083$$

Throughout the world, the ratio that is used most commonly is percent. However, in some countries, you will find both ratios in use.

Express per mill as a decimal.

1. 325‰

2. 71‰

3. 6‰

4. 900‰

5. 20‰

6. 100‰

Express each per mill as a fraction in simplest form.

7. 47‰

8. 400‰

9. 100‰

10. 25‰

11. 150‰

12. 30‰

Express each fraction as a per mill.

13. $\frac{729}{1,000}$

14. $\frac{58}{100}$

15. $\frac{7}{10}$

16. $\frac{1}{2}$

17. $\frac{3}{4}$

18 $\frac{5}{8}$

19. $\frac{4}{5}$

20. $\frac{17}{20}$

21. $\frac{1}{3}$

22. CHALLENGE In the United States, you will sometimes find the **mill** used as a monetary unit. What amount of money do you think is represented by 1 mill?

7-4 Lesson Reading Guide

Probability

Get Ready for the Lesson

Read the introduction at the top of page 381 in your textbook.
Write your answers below.

1. Write a ratio that compares the number of yellow carnations to the total number of carnations.

2. What percent of the carnations are yellow?

3. Does Morgan have a good chance of selecting a yellow carnation?

4. What would happen to her chances of picking a yellow carnation if one each of a green, lilac, orange, dark purple, and teal carnation were added to the flowers shown?

5. What happens to her chances if there is only one yellow carnation and one pink carnation?

Read the Lesson

For Exercises 6–8, see the Key Concept box at the bottom of page 381.

6. In the equation, what does P(event) represent? In terms of the example at the top of the page 381, what is the event?

7. In terms of question 1, what would be a favorable outcome?

8. In terms of the carnations shown, what are the possible outcomes?

9. In Example 4 at the bottom of page 383, how do you read the equation $P(blue\ eyes) + P(not\ blue\ eyes) = 100\%$? What are "blue eyes" and "not blue eyes" called?

Remember What You Learned

10. A bouquet of flowers contains 6 pink roses, 3 purple roses, and 4 red roses. What is the probability that Morgan would pick a purple rose if her eyes were closed? Write an equation using the symbols from the lesson.

Lesson 7-4

7-4 Study Guide and Intervention

Probability

When tossing a coin, there are two possible **outcomes**, heads and tails. Suppose you are looking for heads. If the coin lands on heads, this would be a favorable outcome or **simple event**. The chance that some event will happen (in this case, getting heads) is called **probability**. You can use a ratio to find probability. The probability of an event is a number from 0 to 1, including 0 and 1. The closer a probability is to 1, the more likely it is to happen.

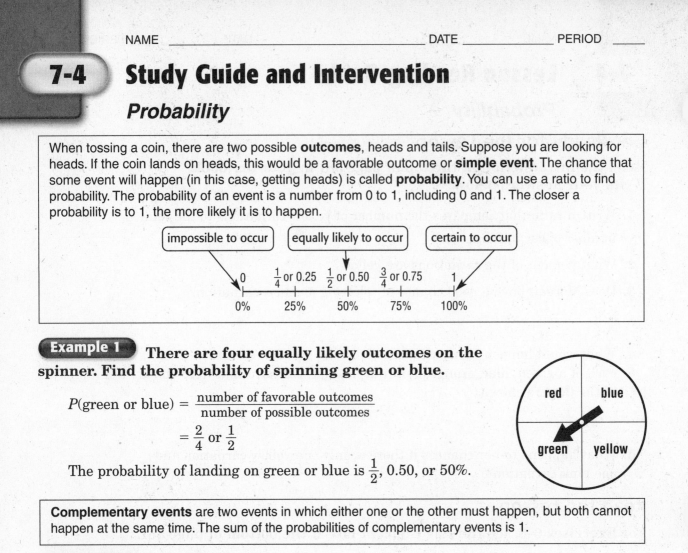

Example 1 There are four equally likely outcomes on the spinner. Find the probability of spinning green or blue.

$$P(\text{green or blue}) = \frac{\text{number of favorable outcomes}}{\text{number of possible outcomes}}$$

$$= \frac{2}{4} \text{ or } \frac{1}{2}$$

The probability of landing on green or blue is $\frac{1}{2}$, 0.50, or 50%.

Complementary events are two events in which either one or the other must happen, but both cannot happen at the same time. The sum of the probabilities of complementary events is 1.

Example 2 There is a 25% chance that Sam will win a prize. What is the probability that Sam will not win a prize?

$$P(\text{win}) + P(\text{not win}) = 1$$
$$0.25 + P(\text{not win}) = 1$$
$$\underline{-0.25 \qquad\qquad = -0.25} \quad \text{Replace } P(\text{win}) \text{ with 0.25.}$$
$$P(\text{not win}) = 0.75 \quad \text{Subtract 0.25 from each side.}$$

So, the probability that Sam won't win a prize is 0.75, 75%, or $\frac{3}{4}$.

Exercises

1. There is a 90% chance that it will rain. What is the probability that it will not rain?

One pen is chosen without looking from a bag that has 3 blue pens, 6 red, and 3 green. Find the probability of each event. Write each answer as a fraction, a decimal, and a percent.

2. $P(\text{green})$ 3. $P(\text{blue or red})$ 4. $P(\text{yellow})$

7-4 Skills Practice

Probability

A card is randomly chosen. Find each probability. Write each answer as a fraction, a decimal, and a percent.

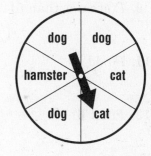

1. $P(B)$

2. $P(Q$ or $R)$

3. $P(\text{vowel})$

4. $P(\text{consonant or vowel})$

5. $P(\text{consonant or A})$

6. $P(T)$

The spinner shown is spun once. Write a sentence explaining how likely it is for each event to occur.

7. $P(\text{dog})$

8. $P(\text{hamster})$

9. $P(\text{dog or cat})$

10. $P(\text{bird})$

11. $P(\text{mammal})$

WEATHER The weather reporter says that there is a 12% chance that it will be moderately windy tomorrow.

12. What is the probability that it will not be windy?

13. Will tomorrow be a good day to fly a kite? Explain.

Lesson 7-4

7-4 **Practice**

Probability

The spinner shown is spun once. Find each probability. Write each answer as a fraction, a decimal, and a percent.

1. $P(C)$

2. $P(G)$

3. $P(M \text{ or } P)$

4. $P(B, E, \text{ or } A)$

5. $P(\text{not vowel})$

6. $P(\text{not } M)$

Eight cards are marked 3, 4, 5, 6, 7, 8, 9, and 10 such that each card has exactly one of these numbers. A card is picked without looking. Find each probability. Write each answer as a fraction, a decimal, and a percent.

7. $P(9)$

8. $P(5 \text{ or } 7)$

9. $P(\text{greater than } 5)$

10. $P(\text{less than } 3)$

11. $P(\text{odd})$

12. $P(4, 7, \text{ or } 8)$

13. $P(\text{not } 6)$

14. $P(\text{not } 5 \text{ and not } 10)$

The spinner is spun once. Write a sentence stating how likely it is for each event to happen. Justify your answer.

15. fish

16. cat

17. bird, cat, or fish

18. PLANTS Of the water lilies in the pond, 43% are yellow. The others are white. A frog randomly jumps onto a lily. Describe the complement of the frog landing on a yellow lily and find its probability.

30

7-4 Word Problem Practice

Probability

Write each answer as a fraction, a decimal, and a percent.

PARTY For Exercises 1 and 2, the spinner shown is spun once. The spinner shows the prizes a person can win at a party.

1. What is the probability that a person will spin a cap? a whistle? a cap or yo-yo?

2. What is the probability that a person will spin a stuffed animal? Explain. What is the probability that a person will win a prize?

3. **WEATHER** The weather report says there is an 85% chance it will be very hot tomorrow. Should you get ready to use the air conditioner? Explain.

4. **EATING HABITS** 7% of Americans are vegetarians. If you ask a random person whether he or she is a vegetarian, what is the probability that the person is *not* a vegetarian? Explain.

5. **SCHOOL** Theresa is taking a multiple-choice test and does not know an answer. She can guess answer A, B, C, D, or E. What is the probability that Theresa will guess correctly? incorrectly?

6. **NUMBER CUBE** You roll a number cube. How likely is it that you will roll a number less than 1? less than 7? Explain.

7. **FOOD** Mrs. Phillips has 10 identical cans without labels. She knows that she had 1 can of peas, 5 cans of corn, 1 can of carrots, and 3 cans of beets. She opens one can. What is the probability it is carrots? corn or beets?

8. In Exercise 7, how likely is it Mrs. Phillips will open a can of corn? a can of peas? Explain.

Lesson 7-4

7-4 Enrichment

Working Backward with Probabilities

Suppose that you are given this information about rolling a number cube.

$$P(1) = \frac{1}{2} \qquad P(3) = \frac{1}{3} \qquad P(5) = \frac{1}{6}$$

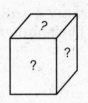

Can you tell what numbers are marked on the faces of the cube? Work backward. Since a cube has six faces, express each probability as a fraction whose denominator is 6.

$$P(1) = \frac{3}{6} \qquad P(3) = \frac{2}{6} \qquad P(5) = \frac{1}{6}$$

So, the cube must have three faces marked with the number 1, two faces marked 3, and one face marked 5.

Each set of probabilities is associated with rolling a number cube. What numbers are marked on the faces of each cube?

1. $P(2) = \frac{1}{3}$

$P(4) = \frac{1}{3}$

$P(6) = \frac{1}{3}$

2. $P(1) = \frac{1}{6}$

$P(4) = \frac{1}{6}$

$P(\text{factor of } 4) = 1$

3. $P(1 \text{ or } 2) = \frac{5}{6}$

$P(2 \text{ or } 3) = \frac{2}{3}$

$P(1, 2, \text{ or } 3) = 1$

Each set of probabilities is associated with the spinner shown at the right. How many sections of each color are there?

4. $P(\text{red}) = \frac{1}{2}$

$P(\text{blue}) = \frac{1}{4}$

$P(\text{green}) = \frac{1}{8}$

$P(\text{black}) = \frac{1}{8}$

5. $P(\text{yellow or purple}) = \frac{5}{8}$

$P(\text{purple or white}) = \frac{3}{4}$

$P(\text{green or blue}) = 0$

$P(\text{yellow, purple, or white}) = 1$

6. Suppose that you are given this information about pulling a marble out of a bag.

$$P(\text{green}) = \frac{1}{4} \qquad P(\text{blue}) = \frac{1}{6} \qquad P(\text{red}) = \frac{3}{8}$$

$$P(\text{yellow}) = \frac{1}{24} \qquad P(\text{white}) = \frac{1}{24} \qquad P(\text{black}) = \frac{1}{8}$$

If the bag contains 48 marbles, how many marbles of each color are there?

7-4 TI-83/84 Plus Activity

Expected and Actual Probability

You can use a TI-83/84 Plus graphing calculator to conduct simulations.

Example Suppose you asked 50 people to choose a number from 0 to 9. Find the expected probability of each possible response or outcome.

Possible Outcome	Expected Frequency	Expected Probability	Possible Outcome	Expected Frequency	Expected Probability
0	5	$\frac{1}{10}$	5	5	$\frac{1}{10}$
1	5	$\frac{1}{10}$	6	5	$\frac{1}{10}$
2	5	$\frac{1}{10}$	7	5	$\frac{1}{10}$
3	5	$\frac{1}{10}$	8	5	$\frac{1}{10}$
4	5	$\frac{1}{10}$	9	5	$\frac{1}{10}$

Instead of asking 50 people, you can simulate the data using a graphing calculator.

Enter: [MATH] [▶] [▶] [▶] [ENTER] [ENTER]

The calculator will display a random decimal. Use the individual digits in the number as if they were responses. Record them in a table like the one below. Repeat this process until you have 50 responses. Find the actual frequency by counting the tallies. Find the actual probability by using the actual frequency.

Outcome	Tally	Actual Frequency	Actual Probability
0			
1			

Exercises

1. Use a graphing calculator to conduct this simulation. Complete the table using your random data. Then find the actual probabilities.

2. Compare your data with those of a friend. Why are they not exactly the same?

Lesson 7-4

7-5   Lesson Reading Guide

Constructing Sample Spaces

Get Ready for the Lesson

**Read the introduction at the top of page 389 in your textbook.
Write your answers below.**

1. List the possible ways to choose a soft drink, a popcorn, and a candy.

2. How do you know you have accounted for all possible combinations?

Read the Lesson

3. In Example 1 on page 389, what is the sample space? What method was used to find the sample space?

4. In the tree diagram in Example 2 on page 390, which part of the diagram shows the sample space?

5. Using the Fundamental Counting Principle in Example 3 on page 390, how do you determine the number of possible outcomes? How many possible outcomes are there?

Remember What You Learned

6. Work with a partner. Think up a situation and use the Fundamental Counting Principle to determine the number of possible outcomes. Then make an organized list, or draw a tree diagram, to determine the sample space.

7-5 Study Guide and Intervention

Constructing Sample Spaces

The **Fundamental Counting Principle** is another way to find the number of possible outcomes. This principle states that if there are m outcomes for a first choice and n outcomes for a second choice, then the total number of possible outcomes can be found by finding $m \times n$.

Example 1 How many sandwiches are possible from a choice of turkey or ham with jack cheese or Swiss cheese?

Draw a tree diagram.

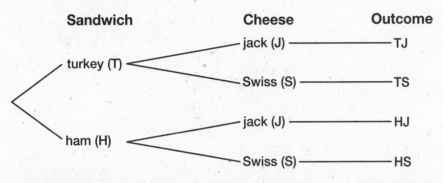

Sandwich	Cheese	Outcome

There are four possible sandwiches.

Example 2 Using the Fundamental Counting Principle, how many sandwiches are possible from a choice of roast beef, turkey, or ham, with a choice of jack, cheddar, American, or Swiss cheese? Find the probability of chossing a ham with jack cheese sandwich.

There are twelve possible sandwiches. To determine the number of possible outcomes, multiply the number of first choices, 3, by the number of second choices, 4, to determine that there are 12 possible outcomes. So, $P(\text{ham, jack}) = \frac{1}{12}$, or 0.083, or 8.3%.

Exercises

First use the Fundamental Counting Principle to determine the number of possible outcomes. Then, check your result and find the sample space by drawing a tree diagram. Finally, find the probability.

1. buy a can or a bottle of grape or orange soda
   Find $P(\text{bottle, grape})$.

2. toss a coin and roll a number cube
   Find $P(4, \text{tails})$.

3. wear jeans or shorts with a blue, white, black, or red T-shirt. Find $P(\text{jeans, white T-shirt})$.

Lesson 7-5

7-5 Skills Practice

Constructing Sample Spaces

1. In how many ways can 2 coins be chosen from a set of 1 penny, 1 nickel, 1 dime, and 1 quarter? Make an organized list to show the sample space.

Use the Fundamental Counting Principle to determine the number of possible outcomes for each situation. Then, draw a tree diagram to show the sample space. Finally, find the given probability.

2. Each spinner is spun once. How many outcomes are possible? Find P(pink, Z).

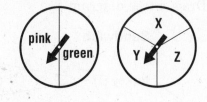

3. chocolate, vanilla, strawberry, or mint ice cream with sugar or waffle cone
   How many outcomes are possible? Find P(vanilla, waffle).

4. paint room cream, violet, or blue with red, white or gold trim
   How many outcomes are possible? Find P(blue, red).

7-5 Practice

Constructing Sample Spaces

1. **SCULPTURE** Diego is lining up driftwood sculptures in front of his woodshop. He has a dolphin, gull, seal, and a whale. In how many different ways can he line up his sculptures? Make an organized list to show the sample space.

2. **CYCLES** A cycle shop sells bicycles, tricycles, and unicycles in a single color of red, blue, green, or white. Draw a tree diagram to find how many different combinations of cycle types and colors are possible.

For Exercises 3–5, a coin is tossed, and the spinners shown are spun.

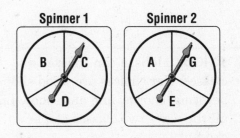

Spinner 1   Spinner 2

3. Using the Fundamental Counting Principle, how many outcomes are possible?

4. What is P(heads, C, G)?

5. Find P(tails, D, a vowel).

Lesson 7-5

7-5 Word Problem Practice

Constructing Sample Spaces

1. **OUTINGS** Olivia and Candace are deciding between Italian or Chinese food and then whether to go to a movie, walk in the park, or go for a bike ride. Using the Fundamental Counting Principle, how many choices do they have?

2. **PETS** Terence is going to get a parrot. He can choose among a yellow, green, or multi-colored female or male parrot. Draw a tree diagram showing all the ways Terence can choose. What is the probability he will choose a yellow female?

3. **CAKE** Julia is ordering a birthday cake. She can have a circular or rectangular chocolate or vanilla cake with chocolate, vanilla, or maple frosting. Draw a tree diagram showing all the possible ways Julia can order her cake. How many options does she have?

4. **GAMES** Todd plays a game in which you toss a coin and roll a number cube. Use the Fundamental Counting Principle to determine the number of possible outcomes. What is P(heads, odd number)?

5. **SCHOOL** Melissa can choose two classes. Her choices are wood shop, painting, chorus, and auto shop. List all the ways two classes can be chosen.

6. **SHOPPING** Kaya has enough allowance to purchase two new baseball caps from the five he likes. How many ways can he choose?

7-5 Enrichment

Listing Outcomes in a Table

Suppose that you spin the two spinners below. What is the probability that the sum of the numbers you spin is 5?

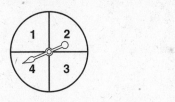

+	1	2	3	4
1	2	3	4	5
2	3	4	5	6
3	4	5	6	7
4	5	6	7	8
5	6	7	8	9
6	7	8	9	10

First Spinner

Second Spinner

To find this probability, you first need to count the outcomes. One way to do this is to use a table of sums like the one at the right. From the table, it is easy to see that there are 24 outcomes. It is also easy to see that, in 4 of these outcomes, the sum of the numbers is 5. So, the probability that the sum of the numbers is 5 is $\frac{4}{24}$, or $\frac{1}{6}$.

Use the spinners and the table above. Find each probability.

1. P(sum is 8)

2. P(sum is 12)

3. P(sum is greater than 6)

4. P(sum is less than or equal to 10)

Suppose you roll two number cubes. Each cube is marked with 1, 2, 3, 4, 5, and 6 on its faces. Find each probability. (*Hint*: On a separate sheet of paper, make a chart like the one above.)

5. P(sum is 9)

6. P(sum is 3)

7. P(sum is an even number)

8. P(sum is a multiple of 3)

9. P(sum is a prime number)

10. P(sum is a factor of 12)

11. P(sum is greater than 12)

12. P(sum is less than 6)

13. **CHALLENGE** Here is a set of probabilities associated with two spinners.

P(sum is 4) $= \frac{1}{6}$ P(sum is 6) $= \frac{1}{3}$

P(sum is 8) $= \frac{1}{3}$ P(sum is 10) $= \frac{1}{6}$

In the space at the right, sketch the two spinners.

Lesson 7-5

7-6 Lesson Reading Guide

Making Predictions

Get Ready for the Lesson

**Complete the Mini Lab at the top of page 394 in your textbook.
Write your answers below.**

1. When working in a group, how did your group predict the number of students in your school with green eyes?

2. Compare your group's prediction with the class prediction. Which do you think is more accurate and why?

Read the Lesson

3. Write the three characteristics of a good sample.

4. Using the characteristics listed above, do you think that a classroom is a good sample of an entire school? Explain.

5. If the question of the survey is, "What is your favorite television program?" would you change the sample in any way? If so, how would you change it?

6. In Examples 1 and 2 on page 395, how is the prediction used?

Remember What You Learned

7. Work with a partner. Find the results of a survey that is of interest to you. For example, to find surveys on favorite TV programs, go to a search engine on the Internet and enter "survey TV programs." Choose one survey. Do you think the survey is a good survey? If so, why? If not, why not and how would you change it?

7-6 Study Guide and Intervention

Making Predictions

A **survey** is a method of collecting information. The group being surveyed is the **population**. To save time and money, part of the group, called a **sample**, is surveyed.

A good sample is:

• selected at **random**, or without preference,

• representative of the population, and

• large enough to provide accurate data.

Examples Every sixth student who walked into the school was asked how he or she got to school.

1 What is the probability that a student at the school rode a bike to school?

School Transportation	
Method	**Students**
walk	10
ride bike	10
ride bus	15
get ride	5

$P(\text{ride bike}) = \dfrac{\text{number of students that rode a bike}}{\text{number of students surveyed}}$

$= \dfrac{10}{40} \text{ or } \dfrac{1}{4}$

So, $P(\text{ride bike}) = \dfrac{1}{4}$, 0.25, or 25%.

2 There are 360 students at the school. Predict how many bike to school.

Write a proportion. Let s = number of students who will ride a bike.

$\dfrac{10}{40} = \dfrac{s}{360}$

You can solve the proportion to find that of the 360 students, 90 will ride a bike to school.

Exercises

SCHOOL Use the following information and the table shown. Every tenth student entering the school was asked which one of the four subjects was his or her favorite.

Favorite Subject	
Subject	**Students**
Language Arts	10
Math	10
Science	15
Social Studies	5

1. Find the probability that any student attending school prefers science.

2. There are 400 students at the school. Predict how many students would prefer science.

7-6 Skills Practice

Making Predictions

Determine whether each sample is a good sample. Explain.

1. 250 people at the beach in the summer are asked to name their favorite vacation spot.

2. Every fourth shopper at a grocery store is asked whether or not he or she owns a pet.

For Exercise 3–6, use the table and the following information. A survey of students' favorite sports was taken from a random sample of students in a school. The results are shown in the table.

Students' Favorite Sports	
Soccer	8
Baseball /Softball	3
Volleyball	5
Track & Field	4

3. What is the size of the sample?

4. What is the probability that a student will prefer soccer?

5. What is the probability that a student will prefer volleyball?

6. There are 550 students in the school. Predict how many students at the school prefer track and field.

For Exercises 7–10, use the table and the following information. A random sample of 40 flower shop customers was surveyed to find customers' favorite flowers. The table shows the results. The shop expects to sell 50 bunches of flowers on Sunday. How many bunches of each flower should the shop order?

Favorite Flower	
Type	Shoppers
Daisy	8
Gardenia	4
Mum	8
Rose	20

7. daisy

8. rose

9. mum

10. gardenia

7-6 Practice

Making Predictions

Lesson 7-6

QUIZ SHOW For Exercises 1 and 2, use the following information.

On a quiz show, a contestant correctly answered 9 of the last 12 questions.

1. Find the probability of the contestant correctly answering the next question.

2. Suppose the contestant continues on the show and tries to correctly answer 24 questions. About how many questions would you predict the contestant to correctly answer?

CHORES For Exercises 3–6, use the table to predict the number of students out of 528 that would say each of the following was their least favorite chore.

Least Favorite Chore	
Chore	**Number of Students**
Clean my room	7
Take out the garbage	4
Wash dishes	5
Walk the dog	3
Vacuum or dust	5

3. clean my room   4. wash dishes

5. walk the dog   6. take out the garbage

7. **SCIENCE** Refer to the bar graph below. A science museum manager asked some of the visitors at random during a typical day which exhibit they preferred. If there are 630 visitors on a typical day, predict the number of visitors who prefer the magnets exhibit. Compare this to the number of visitors who prefer the weather exhibit.

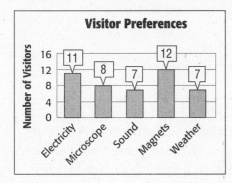

7-6 Word Problem Practice

Making Predictions

MOVIES For Exercises 1–3, use the table of results of Jeremy's survey of favorite kinds of movies.

Favorite Movie Type	
Type	**People**
Drama	12
Foreign	3
Comedy	20
Action	15

SLEEP For Exercises 4–7, use the table of results of the Better Sleep Council's survey of Americans to find the most important factors for good sleep.

Most Important Factors for Good Sleep	
Good Mattress	32
Daily Exercise	20
Good Pillows	8
Healthy Diet	11
Other Factors	29

1. **MOVIES** How many people did Jeremy use for his sample?

2. If Jeremy were to ask any person to name his or her favorite type of movie, what is the probability that it would be comedy?

3. If Jeremy were to survey 250 people, how many would you predict would name comedy?

4. **SLEEP** Predict how many people out of 400 would say that a good mattress is the most important factor.

5. What is the probability that any person chosen at random would not say that a healthy diet is the most important factor?

6. Suppose 250 people were chosen at random. Predict the number of people that would say good pillows are the most important factor.

7. What is the probability that any person chosen at random would say that daily exercise is the most important factor for a good night sleep?

8. **ICE CREAM** Claudia went to an ice cream shop to conduct a survey. She asked every tenth person who entered the shop to name his or her favorite dessert. Did Claudia select a good sample? Explain.

7-6　Enrichment

Odds

People who play games of chance often talk about **odds**. You can find the *odds in favor* of an event by using this formula.

$$\text{odds in favor} = \frac{\text{number of ways an event can occur}}{\text{number of ways the event cannot occur}}$$

With the spinner shown at the right, for example, this is how you would find the odds in favor of the event *prime number*.

There are four prime numbers (2, 3, 5, 7). → $\frac{4}{6} = \frac{2}{3}$
Six numbers are not prime (1, 4, 6, 8, 9, 10). →

The odds in favor of the event *prime number* are $\frac{2}{3}$ or 2 to 3.

Suppose that you spin the spinner shown above. Find the odds in favor of each event.

1. number greater than 3

2. number less than or equal to 6

3. even number

4. odd number

5. multiple of 3

6. factor of 10

To find the *odds against* an event, you use this formula.

$$\text{odds against} = \frac{\text{number of ways an event cannot occur}}{\text{number of ways the event can occur}}$$

Suppose that you roll a number cube with 1, 2, 3, 4, 5, and 6 marked on its faces. Find the odds against each event.

7. number less than 5

8. number greater than or equal to 2

9. even number

10. odd number

11. number divisible by 3

12. factor of 12

13. **CHALLENGE** The probability of an event is $\frac{2}{3}$. What are the odds in favor of the event? the odds against the event?

7-6 Scientific Calculator Activity

Making Predictions Using Samples

Two classes of sixth-grade students were asked to give their favorite brand of athletic shoe. The results are shown at the right.

Find the probability that the favorite brand of athletic shoe of a sixth-grade student is Brand B.

Find the size of the sample.

Enter: 6 $\boxed{+}$ 18 $\boxed{+}$ 11 $\boxed{+}$ 10 $\boxed{\text{ENTER}\atop=}$ 45

The sample size is 45.

Find the probability that the favorite brand is Brand B.

$$P(\text{Brand B}) = \frac{\text{number who chose Brand B}}{\text{size of the sample}}$$

Enter: 18 $\boxed{\div}$ 45 $\boxed{\text{ENTER}\atop=}$ 0.4

The probability that the favorite brand is Brand B is 0.4.

Favorite Brand of Shoe (Number of Students)

Brand A 6
Brand D 10
Brand B 18
Brand C 11

Find the probability of making each of the choices below. Round to the nearest hundredth.

1. survey of sixth-graders' favorite color

   P(red):   P(blue):

   P(green):   P(pink):

   P(black):   P(purple):

2. survey of the favorite sport of sixth graders

   P(soccer):   P(baseball):

   P(basketball):   P(swimming):

   P(hockey):   P(football):

   P(gymnastics):

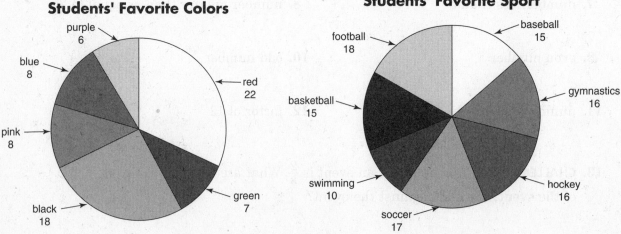

Students' Favorite Colors

purple 6
blue 8
pink 8
black 18
red 22
green 7

Students' Favorite Sport

football 18
baseball 15
basketball 15
gymnastics 16
swimming 10
soccer 17
hockey 16

7-7 Study Guide and Intervention

Problem-Solving Investigation: Solve a Simpler Problem

Lesson 7-7

When solving problems, one strategy that is helpful is to *solve a simpler problem*. Using some of the information presented in the problem, you may be able to set up and solve a simpler problem.

You can use the *solve a simpler problem* strategy, along with the following four-step problem solving plan to solve a problem.

1 Understand – Read and get a general understanding of the problem.

2 Plan – Make a plan to solve the problem and estimate the solution.

3 Solve – Use your plan to solve the problem.

4 Check – Check the reasonableness of your solution.

Example **PUZZLES** Steven and Darshelle are putting together a 500 piece puzzle. So far they have 40% of the puzzle complete. How many pieces are left for them to fit into the puzzle?

Understand We know the total number of pieces in the puzzle and that 40% of the pieces are already put together in the puzzle. We need to find the number of pieces left to fit in the puzzle.

Plan Solve a simpler problem by finding 100% − 40% or 60% of the 500 pieces. First find 10% of 500 and then use the result to find 60% of 500.

Solve Since 10%, or $\frac{1}{10}$ of 500 is 50.

So, 60%, or $\frac{6}{10}$ of 500 is 6 × 50 or 300.

Steven and Darshelle still have 300 pieces left to fit in the puzzle.

Check We know that 40% or 4 out of every 10 pieces of the puzzle are already put together in the puzzle. Since 500 ÷ 10 × 4 = 200 pieces and 200 + 300 = 500, the answer is correct.

Exercise

SCHOLARSHIPS Crosswood Elementary School received $450 in donations for its scholarship fund. If 30% of the contributions were from local businesses, how much money did the local businesses contribute?

7-7 Skills Practice

Problem-Solving Investigation: Solve a Simpler Problem

Solve. Use the solve a simpler problem strategy.

1. **SCHOOLS** A total of 350 students voted on whether a marlin or a panther should be the new school's mascot. If 30% of the students voted for the panther as the mascot, how many of the students voted for the panther?

2. **READING** Over the summer, Maggie plans to read one book the first week and double the number of books each week for the next 5 weeks. How many books will Maggie read in the sixth week?

3. **GEOGRAPHY** The total area of Michigan is 96,810 square miles. Of that, about 40% is water. About how much of Michigan's area is land?

4. **ANIMALS** A spider travels at a speed of 1.17 miles per hour. At this rate, about how far can a spider travel in 3 hours?

7-7 Practice

Problem-Solving Investigation: Solve a Simpler Problem

Mixed Problem Solving

Use the solve a simpler problem strategy to solve Exercises 1–3.

1. **ART** An artist plans to make 1 clay pot the first week and triple the number of clay pots each week for 5 weeks. How many clay pots will the artist make the fifth week?

2. **GEOGRAPHY** The total area of Wisconsin is 65,498 square miles. Of that, about 80% is land area. About how much of Wisconsin is not land area?

3. **SCIENCE** Sound travels through sea water at a speed of about 1,500 meters per second. At this rate, how far will sound travel in 2 minutes?

Use any strategy to solve Exercises 4–8. Some strategies are shown below.

Problem-Solving Strategies
• Guess and check.
• Solve a simpler problem.

4. **MUSIC** Tanya scored 50 out of 50 points in her latest piano playing evaluation. She scored 42, 48, and 45 on previous evaluations. What score does she need on the next evaluation to have an average score of 45?

5. **EXERCISE** At the community center, 9 boys and 9 girls are playing singles table tennis. If each girl plays against each boy exactly once, how many games are played?

6. **CLOCK** The clock in the bell tower rings every half hour. How many times will it ring in one week?

7. **VENN DIAGRAMS** The Venn diagram shows information about the sixth graders in the school.

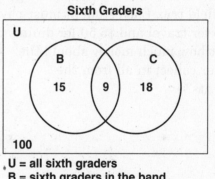

Sixth Graders

U = all sixth graders
B = sixth graders in the band
C = sixth graders in the chorus

How many more sixth graders in the school do not participate in band or chorus than do participate in band or chorus?

8. **MONEY** Kono wants to give $69 to charity. He will give each of 3 charities an equal amount of money. How much money will each charity receive?

7-7 Word Problem Practice

Problem-Solving Investigation: Solve a Simpler Problem

1. FOOD Is $8 enough money to buy a dozen eggs for $1.29, one pound of ground beef for $3.99, and a gallon of milk for $2.09? Explain.

2. SURVEY The circle graph shows the results of a favorite juice survey. What percents best describe the data?

Favorite Juice

3. MONEY A total of 32 students are going on a field trip. Each student must pay $4.75 for travel and $5.50 for dining. About how much money should the teacher collect in all from the students?

4. TRAVEL Mr. Ishikawa left Houston at 3:00 P.M. and arrived in Dallas at 8:00 P.M., driving a distance of approximately 240 miles. During his trip, he took a one-hour dinner break. What was Mr. Ishikawa's average speed?

5. BAKE SALE Oakdale Middle School received 240 contributions for its bake sale. If 30% of the contributions were pies, how many pies did the school receive?

6. BABYSITTING About how much more did Cara earn babysitting in 2008 than in 2007?

Cara's Babysitting Earnings	
Year	Earnings
2006	$98.50
2007	$149.00
2008	$218.75

7-8 Lesson Reading Guide

Estimating with Percents

Get Ready for the Lesson

Complete the Mini Lab at the top of page 401 in your textbook.
Write your answers below.

Use grid paper to find the fractional portion of each number.

1. $\frac{1}{2}$ of 10

2. $\frac{1}{5}$ of 10

3. $\frac{2}{5}$ of 20

4. $\frac{5}{6}$ of 36

5. **MAKE A CONJECTURE** How can you find a fractional part of a number
without drawing a model on grid paper?

Read the Lesson

6. Write the fraction for each percent.

20% =	40% =	60% =	80% =
25% =	50% =	75% =	100% =
$33\frac{1}{3}$% =	$66\frac{2}{3}$% =		

7. Complete the sentence.
   When you estimate with percents, you round to numbers that are
   _____.

Remember What You Learned

8. Work with a partner. Using the fractions and percents in the table you
   completed for Exercise 6, take turns saying either a fraction or percent. If
   you say a fraction, your partner writes the corresponding percent. If you
   say a percent, your partner writes the corresponding fraction. Make sure
   your partner cannot see the table above. Continue with your practice until
   you can remember all the fractions and percents.

7-8 Study Guide and Intervention

Estimating with Percents

The table below shows some commonly used percents and their fraction equivalents.

Percent-Fraction Equivalents				
$20\% = \frac{1}{5}$	$50\% = \frac{1}{2}$	$80\% = \frac{4}{5}$	$25\% = \frac{1}{4}$	$33\frac{1}{3}\% = \frac{1}{3}$
$30\% = \frac{3}{10}$	$60\% = \frac{3}{5}$	$90\% = \frac{9}{10}$	$75\% = \frac{3}{4}$	$66\frac{2}{3}\% = \frac{2}{3}$
$40\% = \frac{2}{5}$	$70\% = \frac{7}{10}$	$100\% = 1$		

Examples **Estimate each percent.**

1 **20% of 58**

20% is $\frac{1}{5}$.

Round 58 to 60 since it is divisible by 5.

$\frac{1}{5}$ of 60 is 12.

So, 20% of 58 is about 12.

2 **76% of 21.**

76% is close to 75% or $\frac{3}{4}$.

Round 21 to 20 since it is divisible by 4.

$\frac{1}{4}$ of 24 is 5.

So $\frac{3}{4}$ of 20 is 3 × 5 or 15

So, 76% of 21 is about 15.

Example 3 **Isabel is reading a book that has 218 pages. She wants to complete 25% of the book by Friday. About how many pages should she read by Friday?**

25% os $\frac{1}{4}$. Round 218 to 200.

$\frac{1}{4}$ of 200 is 50.

So, Isabel should read about 50 pages by Friday.

Exercises

Estimate each percent.

1. 49% of 8

2. 24% of 27

3. 19% of 46

4. 62% of 20

5. 40% of 51

6. 81% of 32

7. TIPS Jodha wants to tip the pizza delivery person about 20%. If the cost of the pizzas is $15.99, what would be a reasonable amount to tip?

7-8 Skills Practice

Estimating with Percents

Estimate each percent.

1. 50% of 39

2. 24% of 13

3. 19% of 31

4. 49% of 71

5. 27% of 81

6. 52% of 118

7. 19% of 94

8. 33% of 61

9. 58% of 5

10. 41% of 10

11. 75% of 17

12. 82% of 24

13. 73% of 61

14. 62% of 34

15. 38% of 42

16. 79% of 16

17. 91% of 82

18. 67% of 241

Estimate the percent of the figure that is shaded.

19.

20.

21.

Lesson 7-8

7-8 Practice

Estimating with Percents

Estimate each percent.

1. 51% of 62   **2.** 39% of 42   **3.** 78% of 148   **4.** 34% of 99

5. 74% of 238   **6.** 70% of 103   **7.** 22% of 152   **8.** 91% of 102

9. 26% of 322   **10.** 65% of 181   **11.** 98% of 60   **12.** 11% of 10

13. Estimate twenty-nine percent of forty-eight.

14. Estimate sixty-two percent of one hundred twenty-four.

Estimate the percent that is shaded in each figure.

15.   **16.**   **17.**

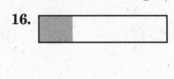

18. WORK Karl made $365 last month doing odd jobs after school. If 75% of the money he made was from doing yard work, about how much did Karl make doing yard work?

19. HOMEWORK Jin spent 32 hours on math and language arts homework last month. She spent 11 hours on math. About what percent of her homework hours were spent on language arts? Explain.

7-8 Word Problem Practice

Estimating with Percents

1. **SCHOOL** At Westside High School, 24% of the 215 sixth grade students walk to school. About how many of the sixth grade students walk to school?

2. **BASKETBALL** In a recent regular season the WNBA Houston Comets won 54.76% of their games. They had 42 games in their regular season. About how many games did they win?

3. **SALES TAX** The sales tax rate in Lacon is 9%. About how much tax would you pay on an item that costs $61?

4. **SPORTS** The concession stand at a football game served 178 customers. Of those, about 52% bought a hot dog. About how many customers bought a hot dog?

5. **SLEEP** A recent study shows that people spend about 31% of their time asleep. About how much time will a person spend asleep during an average 78 year lifetime?

6. **BIOLOGY** The human body is 72% water, on average. About how much water will be in a person that weighs 138 pounds?

7. **MONEY** A video game that originally costs $25.99 is on sale for 50% off. If you have $14, would you have enough money to buy the video game?

8. **SHOPPING** A store is having a 20% sale. That means the customer pays 80% of the regular price. If you have $33, will you have enough money to buy an item that regularly sells for $44.99? Explain.

Lesson 7–8

7-8 Enrichment

Using 100%, 10%, and 1%

Many people think of 100%, 10%, and 1% as *key percents*.

100% is the **whole**.   100% of 24 = 1 × 24, or 24.

10% is **one tenth** of the whole.   10% of 24 = 0.1 × 24, or 2.4.

1% is **one hundredth** of the whole.   1% of 24 = 0.01 × 24, or 0.24.

Find the percent of each number.

1. 100% of 8,000   **2.** 10% of 8,000

3. 1% of 8,000   **4.** 10% of 640

5. 100% of 720   **6.** 1% of 290

7. 1% of 50   **8.** 100% of 33

9. 10% of 14   **10.** 100% of 2

11. 1% of 9   **12.** 10% of 7

This is how you can use the key percents to make some computations easier.

3% of 610 = ___?___.   5% of 24 = ___?___.

1% of 610 = 6.1,   10% of 24 = 2.4,

so 3% of 610 = 3 × 6.1, or 18.3.   so 5% of 24 = $\frac{1}{2}$ of 2.4, or 1.2.

Find the percent of each number.

13. 2% of 140   **14.** 8% of 2,100

15. 4% of 9   **16.** 20% of 233

17. 70% of 90   **18.** 30% of 4,110

19. 5% of 160   **20.** 5% of 38

21. 50% of 612   **22.** 25% of 168

23. 2.5% of 320   **24.** 2.5% of 28

7 Student Recording Sheet

Use this recording sheet with pages 412–413 of the Student Edition.

Part 1: Multiple Choice

Read each question. Then fill in the correct answer.

1. Ⓐ Ⓑ Ⓒ Ⓓ   4. Ⓕ Ⓖ Ⓗ Ⓘ   7. Ⓐ Ⓑ Ⓒ Ⓓ

2. Ⓕ Ⓖ Ⓗ Ⓘ   5. Ⓐ Ⓑ Ⓒ Ⓓ   8. Ⓕ Ⓖ Ⓗ Ⓘ

3. Ⓐ Ⓑ Ⓒ Ⓓ   6. Ⓕ Ⓖ Ⓗ Ⓘ   9. Ⓐ Ⓑ Ⓒ Ⓓ

Part 2: Short Response/Grid in

Record your answer in the blank.

For grid in questions, also enter your answer in the grid by writing each number or symbol in a box. Then fill in the corresponding circle for that number or symbol.

10. _____ (grid in)

11. _____ (grid in)

10.   11.

Part 3: Extended Response

Record your answers for Question 12 on the back of this paper.

Assessment

Rubric for Scoring Extended Response SCORE _____

(Use to score the Extended-Response question on page 413 of the Student Edition.)

General Scoring Guidelines

- If a student gives only a correct numerical answer to a problem but does not show how he or she arrived at the answer, the student will be awarded only 1 credit. All extended response questions require the student to show work.

- A fully correct answer for a multiple-part question requires correct responses for all parts of the question. For example, if a question has three parts, the correct response to one or two parts of the question that required work to be shown is *not* considered a fully correct response.

- Students who use trial and error to solve a problem must show their method. Merely showing that the answer checks or is correct is not considered a complete response for full credit.

Exercise 12 Rubric

Score	Specific Criteria
4	An accurate tree diagram listing all of the combinations is drawn. An understanding that there would be 9 fewer combinations if the mauve shirt were removed from the choices is demeonstrated. An understanding that choosing the given combination consisting of a shirt, hat, and pair of socks at random is $\frac{2}{27}$.
3	An understanding of how the removal of a choice of shirt would affect the number of choices is demonstrated, and the probability is correct, but there are one or two mistakes on the tree diagram.
2	The tree diagram is correct, but an understanding of how the removal of a choice of shirt would affect the number of combinations is not demonstrated, and the probability is incorrect.
1	An understanding of how the removal of a choice of shirt would affect the number of combinations is demonstrated, but the probability and tree diagram are incorrect. **OR** The probability is correct, but an understanding of how the removal of a choice of shirt would affect the number of combinations is not demonstrated, and the tree diagram is incorrect.
0	Response is completely incorrect.

7 Chapter 7 Quiz 1

(Lessons 7-1 and 7-2)

SCORE _____

Write each percent as a fraction in simplest form.

1. 5% **2.** 130% **3.** 40%

1. _____

2. _____

3. _____

Write each fraction as a percent.

4. $\dfrac{9}{20}$ **5.** $\dfrac{5}{2}$ **6.** $\dfrac{1}{5}$

4. _____

5. _____

6. _____

Favorite Subject

English 5%
Social Studies 12%
Math 28%
Science 12%
Art 21%
Gym 22%

SURVEYS Refer to the circle graph that shows results from a World Almanac for Kids online poll.

7. Which subject is the most popular?

8. Which two subjects combined received half of the votes?

7. _____

8. _____

- -

7 Chapter 7 Quiz 2

(Lessons 7-3 and 7-4)

SCORE _____

Write each percent as a decimal.

1. 21% **2.** 0.4%

1. _____

2. _____

Write each decimal as a percent.

3. 0.35 **4.** 0.812

3. _____

4. _____

Replace each ● with <, >, or = to make a true sentence.

5. 13% ● 1.3% **6.** 5.1% ● 15%

5. _____

6. _____

For Questions 7–10, a set of 8 cards is numbered 1 to 8. One card is chosen without looking. Find the probability of each event. Write each answer as a fraction, a decimal and a percent.

7. $P(4)$ **8.** $P(1 \text{ or } 2)$

9. $P(\text{greater than } 5)$ **10.** $P(\text{not } 5)$

7. _____

8. _____

9. _____

10. _____

Assessment

7 Chapter 7 Quiz 3

(Lessons 7-5 and 7-6)

1. **PARADE** For the annual Fourth of July parade, Tomas has a choice of a red, white, or blue wig for his head and tennis shoes, roller skates, or stilts for his feet. Draw a tree diagram of the sample space. Then tell how many outcomes are possible.

1. _____

2. **MUSIC** A band is selling three different concerts on CD or DVD. Draw a tree diagram to show the sample space. Then tell how many outcomes are possible.

2. _____

3. **FOOD** Mica surveyed the fifth grade class about their favorite cafeteria lunch. Use the table at the right to predict the number of students out of the 372 that would prefer spaghetti.

Favorite Cafeteria Lunch	
Lunch	**Students**
Pizza	25
Tacos	12
Spaghetti	10
Cheeseburgers	13

SOCCER Yoko scored 4 goals in her first 12 attempts.

3. _____

4. What is the probability that Yoko will score a goal on her next attempt?

4. _____

5. Suppose Yoko attempts to score 30 goals. About how many goals will she make?

5. _____

- -

7 Chapter 7 Quiz 4

(Lessons 7-7 and 7-8)

1. **MONEY** Darlene wants to give her hair dresser a 20% tip. If her haircut cost $38.50, about how much money should she pay all together?

1. _____

Estimate each percent.

2. 69% of 140   3. 47% of 82   4. 26% of 119

2. _____

3. _____

5. **MULTIPLE-CHOICE** Which of the following is a reasonable percent for the percent of of the figure that is shaded?

4. _____

   A. 25%   C. 50%

   B. 30%   D. 65%

5. _____

60

7 Chapter 7 Mid-Chapter Test

SCORE _____

(Lessons 7-1 through 7-4)

PART I

Write the letter for the correct answer in the blank at the right of each question.

1. **BASKETBALL** Lelia makes $\frac{7}{8}$ of her free throws. What is Lelia's free-throw percentage?

   A. 70% **B.** 80% **C.** 87.5% **D.** 95% 1. _____

FOOD Refer to the circle graph.

Favorite Sandwich

2. What sandwich is the most popular?

   F. tuna **H.** bologna
   G. peanut butter **J.** cheese 2. _____

3. Which two sandwiches are equal in popularity?

   A. tuna and bologna **C.** cheese and bologna
   B. cheese and tuna **D.** tuna and peanut butter 3. _____

   Tuna 25% | Peanut Butter 33% | Grilled Cheese 21% | Bologna 21%

4. Write 2.45 as a percent.

   F. 0.0245% **G.** 0.245% **H.** 2.45% **J.** 245% 4. _____

5. Which of the following could *not* represent the probability of an event?

   A. 1 **B.** 0.5 **C.** 47.9% **D.** $\frac{45}{7}$ 5. _____

PART II

Write each percent as a fraction in simplest form. 6. _____

6. 35% 7. 120% 7. _____

Write each fraction or mixed number as a percent. 8. _____

8. $\frac{3}{10}$ 9. $\frac{13}{4}$ 9. _____

Write each percent as a decimal. 10. _____

10. 48% 11. 6% 11. _____

Write each decimal as a percent. 12. _____

12. 0.65 13. 3.02 13. _____

A set of 10 cards is numbered 1–10. One card is chosen without looking. Find the probability of each event. Write each answer as a fraction, a decimal, and a percent. 14. _____

14. *P*(6) 15. *P*(not 4) 15. _____

Assessment

7 Chapter 7 Vocabulary Test

circle graphs	probability	survey
complementary events	random	tree diagram
outcomes	sample	Fundamental Counting Principle
percent	sample space	
population	simple event	

Choose the correct term or phrase to complete each sentence.

1. Outcomes are possible (results, questions).

1. _____

2. A (sample, population) is part of the group being studied.

2. _____

3. An event is (any possible, a favorable) outcome.

3. _____

4. A tree diagram is a diagram that gives (a random, an organized) list of outcomes.

4. _____

5. A (sample, sample space) is the set of all possible outcomes.

5. _____

6. A (percent, rate) is a ratio that compares a number to 100.

6. _____

7. *Random* means (with, without) preference.

7. _____

8. A population is (the entire, part of the) group being studied in a survey.

8. _____

9. (Population, Complementary) events are two events in which either one or the other must happen, but they cannot happen at the same time.

9. _____

10. A (tree diagram, survey) is a method of collecting information consisting of questions that require a response.

10. _____

11. The Fundamental Counting Principle can be used to determine the (probability, sample space) of an event.

11. _____

In your own words, define the term.

12. circle graph

12. _____

7 Chapter 7 Test, Form 1

SCORE _____

Write the letter for the correct answer in the blank at the right of each question.

1. Write 60% as a fraction in simplest form.

   A. $\frac{60}{100}$ **B.** $\frac{30}{50}$ **C.** $\frac{15}{25}$ **D.** $\frac{3}{5}$ 1. _____

2. Write $\frac{3}{20}$ as a percent.

   F. 18%   **G.** 60%   **H.** 15%   **J.** 66.7%   2. _____

FOOD Refer to the circle graph.

Favorite Fruit

3. Which fruit is most popular?

   A. apple   **C.** banana
   B. peach   **D.** orange   3. _____

4. Which fruit is least popular?

   F. apple   **H.** banana
   G. peach   **J.** orange   4. _____

Orange 30% Apple 36% Peach 9% Banana 25%

5. Write 15% as a decimal.

   A. 0.015   **B.** 150   **C.** 0.15   **D.** 15   5. _____

6. Write 0.02 as a percent.

   F. 0.0002%   **G.** 2%   **H.** 20%   **J.** 0.02%   6. _____

7. A number card from 1 to 5 is picked at random. What is $P(1)$?

   A. 1   **B.** 20%   **C.** 0.25   **D.** $\frac{1}{6}$ 7. _____

8. A 6-sided number cube is rolled. What is $P(\text{less than } 4)$?

   F. 3   **G.** 60%   **H.** 0.5   **J.** $\frac{1}{3}$ 8. _____

For Questions 9–12, use the following information. A set of 10 cards is numbered 1 to 10. One card is chosen without looking.

9. What is $P(5)$?

   A. 5   **B.** 1   **C.** $\frac{1}{2}$ **D.** $\frac{1}{10}$ 9. _____

10. What is $P(2 \text{ or } 3)$?

    F. 2   **G.** $\frac{1}{5}$ **H.** $\frac{1}{6}$ **J.** $\frac{1}{10}$ 10. _____

11. What is $P(\text{even})$?

    A. 5   **B.** 1   **C.** $\frac{1}{2}$ **D.** $\frac{1}{10}$ 11. _____

12. What is $P(\text{not } 10)$?

    F. 0   **G.** 9   **H.** $\frac{9}{10}$ **J.** $\frac{1}{10}$ 12. _____

Assessment

7 Chapter 7 Test, Form 1 *(continued)*

13. **SHOPPING** A store carries nylon and leather backpacks, in either blue, green, or red. Use a tree diagram to find the number of different backpacks.

    A. 3   **B.** 5   **C.** 6   **D.** 8   **13.** _____

14. A red, a blue, a green, and a yellow marble are in a bag. Use the Fundamental Counting Principle to find how many different ways a person can choose 2 marbles from the bag.

    F. 6   **G.** 12   **H.** 4   **J.** 3   **14.** _____

SOCCER Nina scored 3 goals in her first 9 attempts.

15. What is the probability that Nina will score a goal on her next attempt?

    A. $\frac{1}{4}$ **B.** $\frac{4}{10}$ **C.** $\frac{1}{3}$ **D.** $\frac{1}{9}$ **15.** _____

16 Nina attempts to score 18 goals. About how many goals will she make?

    F. 3   **G.** 6   **H.** 10   **J.** 12   **16.** _____

Ben surveyed the students in his class to find which day of the weekend they like the best. The table at the right shows the survey results.

Favorite Weekend Day	
Day	**Students**
Saturday	10
Sunday	8
Not sure	2

17. A student is picked at random. What is the probability that he or she likes Saturday the best?

    A. 20%   **B.** $\frac{1}{2}$ **C.** $\frac{2}{5}$ **D.** $\frac{1}{10}$ **17.** _____

18. Ben's school has 200 students. Predict how many of the students like Sunday the best.

    F. 100   **G.** 80   **H.** 160   **J.** 120   **18.** _____

Estimate each percent.

19. 25% of 395

    A. 10   **B.** 100   **C.** 1,000   **D.** 1,600   **19.** _____

20. 48% of 60

    F. 3,000   **G.** 300   **H.** 3   **J.** 30   **20.** _____

Bonus What percent of the rectangle is shaded?   **B:** _____

Copyright © Glencoe/McGraw-Hill, a division of The McGraw-Hill Companies, Inc.

Write the letter for the correct answer in the blank at the right of each question.

1. Write 154% as a fraction in simplest form.
   A. $\frac{100}{154}$ B. $\frac{50}{77}$ C. $1\frac{27}{50}$ D. $\frac{27}{50}$ 1. _____

2. Write $\frac{17}{20}$ as a percent.
   F. 85%   G. 17%   H. 34%   J. 95%   2. _____

FOOD Refer to the circle graph.

Tropical Smoothie

3. What is the main ingredient?
   A. banana
   B. pineapple
   C. yogurt
   D. ice   3. _____

4. Which two ingredients make up more than half of a Tropical Smoothie?
   F. ice and banana   H. banana and orange
   G. banana and yogurt   J. yogurt and ice   4. _____

5. Write 141% as a decimal.
   A. 14.1   B. 1.41   C. 0.141   D. 141   5 _____

6. Write 0.054 as a percent.
   F. 5.4%   G. 54%   H. 0.00054%   J. 0.54%   6. _____

7. Which percent is greater than 0.4?
   A. 29%   B. 42%   C. 39%   D. 25%   7. _____

8. Which of the following could *not* represent the probability of an event?
   F. 0   G. 0.67   H. 47.9   J. $\frac{7}{34}$ 8. _____

9. A number card from 1 to 8 is randomly chosen. What is $P(5)$?
   A. 1   B. 12%   C. 0.125   DI. $\frac{5}{8}$ 9. _____

10. A number cube is rolled. What is P(greater than 2)?
    F. 4   G. $66.\overline{6}\%$ H. 0.5   J. $\frac{1}{3}$ 10. _____

7   Chapter 7 Test, Form 2A   *(continued)*

GAMES For Questions 11–16, use the table. A carnival has a tub of ducks with colored stickers on the bottom. Each player chooses one duck without looking and then replaces it.

Color	Number	Prize
Red	14	Small
Blue	8	Medium
White	2	Large

11. What is the probability of winning a small prize?

    A. 14%   **B.** 1   **C.** $\frac{7}{12}$ **D.** $\frac{1}{3}$ 11. _____

12. What is the probability of *not* winning a large prize?

    F. 98%   **G.** $\frac{1}{12}$ **H.** $\frac{11}{12}$ **J.** $\frac{23}{24}$ 12. _____

13. What is the probability of winning a large or a medium prize?

    A. 10%   **B.** $\frac{5}{12}$ **C.** $\frac{5}{24}$ **D.** $\frac{14}{24}$ 13. _____

14. Out of 18 plays, predict how many people will win a medium prize.

    F. 10   **G.** 9   **H.** 6   **J.** 2   14. _____

15. If 204 prizes are bought, how many should be medium prizes?

    A. 102   **B.** 68   **C.** 100   **D.** 51   15. _____

16. If Kent plays two separate times, what is the probability he wins a small prize both times?

    F. 28%   **G.** $\frac{28}{144}$ **H.** $\frac{49}{144}$ **J.** $\frac{2}{48}$ 16. _____

17. A red, a blue, a green, a yellow, and an orange marble are in a bag. Use the Fundamental Counting Principle to find how many different ways a person can choose 2 marbles from the bag.

    A. 25   **B.** 10   **C.** 16   **D.** 125   17. _____

18. **FOOD** For breakfast, Mateo can have an onion, garlic, sesame, or poppy seed bagel with cream cheese or butter. Use a tree diagram to find how many outcomes are possible.

    F. 4   **G.** 6   **H.** 8   **J.** 16   18. _____

Estimate each percent.

19. 49% of 598

    A. 3   **B.** 30   **C.** 300   **D.** 3,000   19. _____

20. 21% of 387

    F. 80   **G.** 0.8   **H.** 800   **J.** 8   20. _____

Bonus Draw a spinner with three colors—blue, red, and yellow—so that the probability of landing on yellow is 0.4 and the probability of landing on blue is 0.2.

    B: _____

Write the letter for the correct answer in the blank at the right of each question.

1. Write 172% as a fraction in simplest form.

   A. $\frac{172}{100}$ **B.** $\frac{8}{25}$ **C.** $1\frac{25}{18}$ **D.** $1\frac{18}{25}$ 1. _____

2. Write $\frac{17}{25}$ as a percent.

   F. 17%   **G.** 34%   **H.** 50%   **J.** 68%   2. _____

FOOD **Refer to the circle graph.**

Summer Smoothie

3. What is the main ingredient?

   A. ice   **C.** milk

   B. watermelon   **D.** blackberry   3. _____

Watermelon 30%

Milk 25%

Orange 12%

Ice 18%

Blackberry 15%

4. Which two ingredients make up more than half of a Summer Smoothie?

   F. watermelon and ice

   G. milk and watermelon

   H. milk, ice, and blackberry

   J. blackberry and milk   4. _____

5. Write 3.8% as a decimal.

   A. 0.038   **B.** 380   **C.** 0.38   **D.** 38   5. _____

6. Write 2.4 as a percent.

   F. 2.4%   **G.** 24%   **H.** 0.024%   **J.** 240%   6. _____

7. Which percent is greater than 0.19?

   A. 25%   **B.** 18%   **C.** 0.2%   **D.** 10%   7. _____

8. Which of the following could *not* represent the probability of an event?

   F. 0.33%   **G.** 1.06   **H.** 0   **J.** $\frac{9}{37}$ 8. _____

9. A number card from 1 to 8 is randomly chosen. What is $P(3)$?

   A. 1   **B.** 12.5%   **C.** 0.128   **D.** $\frac{3}{8}$ 9. _____

10. A number cube is rolled. What is $P(\text{less than } 5)$?

    F. 4   **G.** 50%   **H.** $0.\overline{6}$ **J.** $\frac{1}{3}$ 10. _____

Assessment

7 **Chapter 7 Test, Form 2B** *(continued)*

GAMES For Questions 11–16, use the table.
A carnival has a tub of ducks with colored
stickers on the bottom. Each player chooses
one duck without looking and then replaces it.

Color	Number	Prize
Red	16	Small
Blue	12	Medium
White	8	Large

11. What is the probability of winning a small prize?

    A. 16%   **B.** 1   **C.** $\frac{16}{39}$ **D.** $\frac{4}{9}$ **11.** _____

12. What is the probability of *not* winning a large prize?

    F. 92%   **G.** $\frac{2}{9}$ **H.** $\frac{7}{36}$ **J.** $\frac{7}{9}$ **12.** _____

13. What is the probability of winning a large or a medium prize?

    A. 20%   **B.** $\frac{5}{36}$ **C.** $\frac{5}{9}$ **D.** 0.55   **13.** _____

14. Out of 12 plays, predict how many people will win a medium prize.

    F. 1   **G.** 2   **H.** 3   **J.** 4   **14.** _____

15. If 234 prizes are bought, how many should be medium prizes?

    A. 117   **B.** 100   **C.** 78   **D.** 52   **15.** _____

16. If Dean plays two separate times, what is the probability he wins a small prize both times?

    F. 32%   **G.** $\frac{8}{36}$ **H.** $\frac{8}{72}$ **J.** $\frac{16}{81}$ **16.** _____

17. A red, a blue, a green, a yellow, an orange, and a purple marble are in a bag. Use the Fundamental Counting Principle to find how many different ways a person can choose 2 marbles from the bag.

    A. 6   **B.** 12   **C.** 15   **D.** 36   **17.** _____

18. FOOD For lunch, Robin can have a peanut butter, tuna, or bologna sandwich with potato chips, corn chips, or pretzels. Use a tree diagram to find how many outcomes are possible.

    F. 3   **G.** 6   **H.** 9   **J.** 12   **18.** _____

Estimate each percent.

19. 24% of 398

    A. 10   **B.** 100   **C.** 1,000   **D.** 0.1   **19.** _____

20. 48% of 159

    F. 80   **G.** 8   **H.** 0.8   **J.** 8,000   **20.** _____

Bonus Draw a spinner with three colors—blue, red, and yellow—so that the probability of landing on yellow is 0.6 and the probability of landing on blue is 0.2.   **B:**

7 Chapter 7 Test, Form 2C

1. Write 82% as a fraction in simplest form.

1. _____

2. Write $\frac{4}{5}$ as a percent.

2. _____

POLLS For Questions 3–5, refer to the circle graph that shows the result of an online poll.

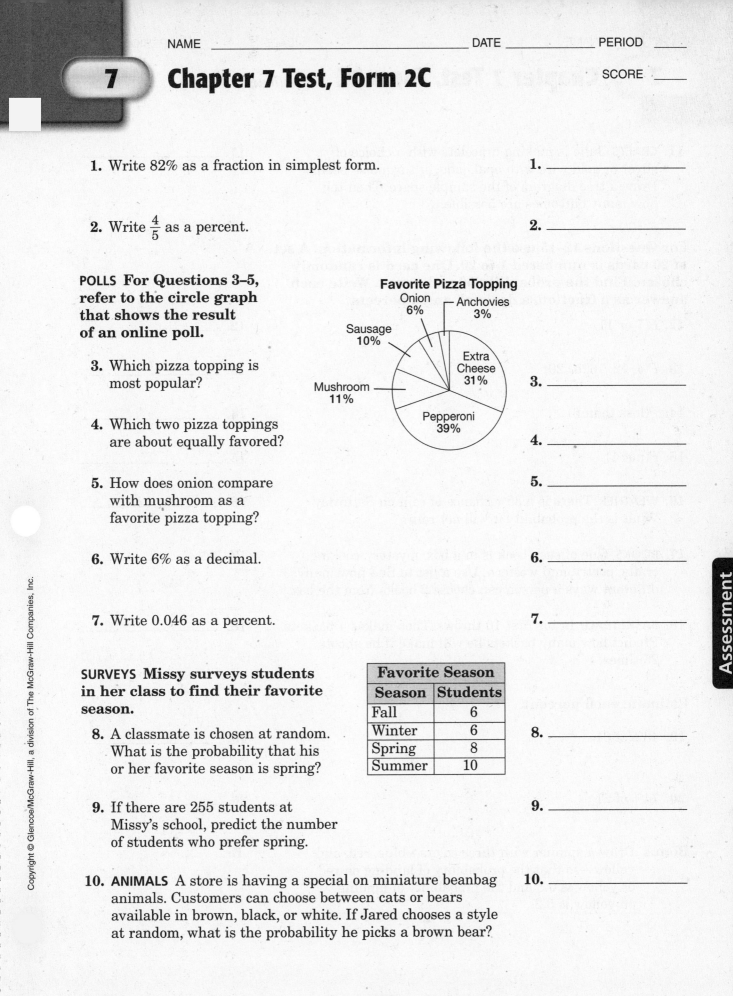

Favorite Pizza Topping

Onion 6%
Anchovies 3%
Sausage 10%
Extra Cheese 31%
Mushroom 11%
Pepperoni 39%

3. Which pizza topping is most popular?

3. _____

4. Which two pizza toppings are about equally favored?

4. _____

5. How does onion compare with mushroom as a favorite pizza topping?

5. _____

6. Write 6% as a decimal.

6. _____

7. Write 0.046 as a percent.

7. _____

SURVEYS Missy surveys students in her class to find their favorite season.

Favorite Season	
Season	**Students**
Fall	6
Winter	6
Spring	8
Summer	10

8. A classmate is chosen at random. What is the probability that his or her favorite season is spring?

8. _____

9. If there are 255 students at Missy's school, predict the number of students who prefer spring.

9. _____

10. **ANIMALS** A store is having a special on miniature beanbag animals. Customers can choose between cats or bears available in brown, black, or white. If Jared chooses a style at random, what is the probability he picks a brown bear?

10. _____

Assessment

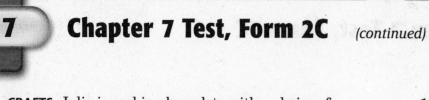
11. **CRAFTS** Julie is making bracelets with a choice of silver or gold wire with opal, jade, or turquoise beads. Draw a tree diagram of the sample space. Then tell how many outcomes are possible.

11. _____

For Questions 12–15 use the following information. A set of 20 cards is numbered 1 to 20. One card is randomly chosen. Find the probability of each event. Write each answer as a fraction, a decimal, and a percent.

12. P(7 or 11)

12. _____

13. P(4, 12, 16, or 20)

13. _____

14. P(less than 6)

14. _____

15. P(not 1)

15. _____

16. **WEATHER** There is a 35% chance of rain on Saturday. What is the probability it will *not* rain?

16. _____

17. **BOOKS** One of each book is in a box: mystery, cooking, crafts, poetry, and western. Use a list to find how many different ways a person can choose 2 books from the box.

17. _____

18. **BASKETBALL** In his first 10 throws, Theo makes 4 baskets. Predict how many baskets he will make if he shoots 25 times.

18. _____

Estimate each percent.

19. 48% of 61

19. _____

20. 74% of 21

20. _____

Bonus Draw a spinner with three colors—blue, red, and yellow—so that the probability of landing on red or yellow is 0.8 and the probability of landing on yellow is 0.2.

B: _____

7 **Chapter 7 Test, Form 2D**

SCORE _____

1. Write 12% as a fraction in simplest form.

1. _____

2. Write $\frac{3}{5}$ as a percent.

2. _____

POLLS Refer to the circle graph that shows the result of an online poll.

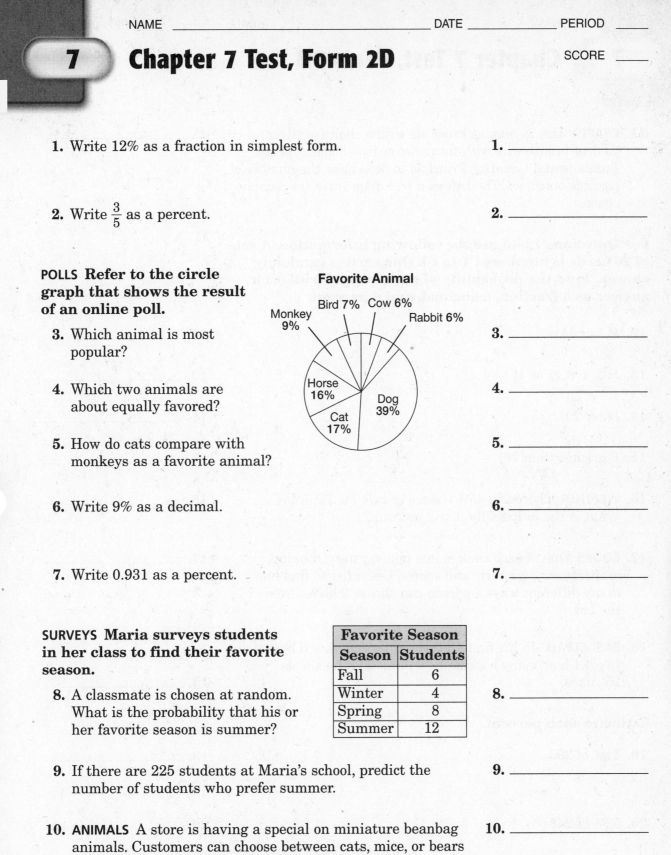

Favorite Animal

Monkey 9%
Bird 7%
Cow 6%
Rabbit 6%
Horse 16%
Cat 17%
Dog 39%

3. Which animal is most popular?

3. _____

4. Which two animals are about equally favored?

4. _____

5. How do cats compare with monkeys as a favorite animal?

5. _____

6. Write 9% as a decimal.

6. _____

7. Write 0.931 as a percent.

7. _____

SURVEYS Maria surveys students in her class to find their favorite season.

Favorite Season	
Season	Students
Fall	6
Winter	4
Spring	8
Summer	12

8. A classmate is chosen at random. What is the probability that his or her favorite season is summer?

8. _____

9. If there are 225 students at Maria's school, predict the number of students who prefer summer.

9. _____

10. **ANIMALS** A store is having a special on miniature beanbag animals. Customers can choose between cats, mice, or bears available in pink or blue. If Julian chooses a style at random, what is the probability he picks a blue bear?

10. _____

7 **Chapter 7 Test, Form 2D** *(continued)*

11. **CRAFTS** Jane is making bracelets with a choice of silver, gold, or bronze wire with turquoise or jade beads. Use the Fundamental Counting Principle to determine the number of possible outcomes. Then, draw a tree diagram of the sample space.

11. _____

For Questions 12–15 use the following information. A set of 20 cards is numbered 1 to 20. One card is randomly chosen. Find the probability of each event. Write each answer as a fraction, a decimal, and a percent.

12. $P(1 \text{ or } 11)$

12. _____

13. $P(2, 4, 6, 8, \text{ or } 10)$

13. _____

14. $P(not\ 20)$

14. _____

15. $P(\text{greater than } 16)$

15. _____

16. **WEATHER** There is a 45% chance of rain on Saturday. What is the probability it will *not* rain?

16. _____

17. **BOOKS** One of each book is in a box: mystery, cooking, crafts, poetry, western, and sports. Use a list to find how many different ways a person can choose 2 books from the box.

17. _____

18. **BASKETBALL** In his first 10 throws, Theo makes 6 baskets. Predict how many baskets he will make if he shoots 25 times.

18. _____

Estimate each percent.

19. 41% of 203

19. _____

20. 52% of 248

20. _____

Bonus Draw a spinner with three colors—blue, red, and yellow—so that the probability of landing on red or blue is 0.6 and the probability of landing on red is 0.2.

B:

7 Chapter 7 Test, Form 3

SCORE _____

Write each percent as a decimal and as a fraction in simplest form.

1. 6%

1. _____

2. 0.8%

2. _____

3. 230%

3. _____

Write each fraction or decimal as a percent.

4. $\frac{16}{25}$

4. _____

5. $\frac{28}{50}$

5. _____

6. 0.15

6. _____

COMPUTERS Refer to the circle graph.

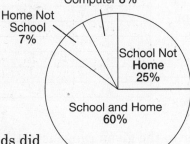

Computer Use by 10- to 13-year-olds

Does Not Use Computer 8%
Home Not School 7%
School Not Home 25%
School and Home 60%

7. What total percent of kids used a computer at home?

7. _____

8. What percent of kids used a computer only at school?

8. _____

9. What total percent of kids did *not* use a computer at home?

9. _____

10. What total percent of kids used a computer?

10. _____

For Questions 11–15 use the following information. A set of 12 cards is numbered 1 to 12. One card is randomly chosen. Find the probability of each event. Write each answer as a fraction, a decimal, and a percent.

11. P(1 or 5)

11. _____

12. P(multiple of 3)

12. _____

13. P(*not* greater than 6)

13. _____

14. P(*not* 1)

14. _____

15. P(less than 13)

15. _____

Assessment

7 **Chapter 7 Test, Form 3** *(continued)*

16. **WEATHER** There is a 30% chance of rain on Saturday and a 40% chance on Sunday. What is the probability it will not rain at all on the weekend?

16. _____

17. How many different ways can a person choose 3 out of 5 markers?

17. _____

18. **POPCORN** By experimenting, Dave finds that 96% of his popcorn kernels pop when he cooks them. If he cooks 125 kernels, predict how many will *not* pop.

18. _____

19. **FOOD** On the nightly special, you can order lasagna, spaghetti, or ravioli, with green salad, soup, or garlic bread. Use the Fundamental Counting Principle to determine the number of possible outcomes. Then, draw a tree diagram of the sample space.

19. _____

SURVEYS Tessa surveys students in her class to find their favorite number less than 8.

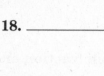

Favorite Number	
Number	Students
1	4
2	5
3	2
4	1
5	5
6	1
7	12

20. A classmate is chosen at random. What is the probability that his or her favorite number is less than 5?

20. _____

21. If there are 420 students at Tessa's school, predict the number of students whose favorite number in the given range is not 7.

21. _____

22. **SHOPPING** A store has green, blue, yellow, and orange socks in either cotton or poly-blend. If Josh's mom picks one style at random, what is the probability she will pick a green or blue cotton pair?

22. _____

Estimate each percent.

23. 32% of 19

23. _____

24. 76% of 123

24. _____

25. **SALES TAX** The sales tax is 8.5%. Estimate how much tax will be charged for a purchase totaling $42.99.

25. _____

Bonus In a board game, two number cubes are rolled at the same time. Each game, every player gets 30 rolls. Predict how many times in one game a player will roll "doubles" (where the same number is rolled on both cubes).

B: _____

7 Chapter 7 Extended-Response Test

Demonstrate your knowledge by giving a clear, concise solution to each problem. Be sure to include all relevant drawings and justify your answers. You may show your solution in more than one way or investigate beyond the requirements of the problem. If necessary, record your answer on another piece of paper.

1. A store is marking merchandise down for the back-to-school sale. Clothing is to be marked down 30%. School supplies are to be on sale for $\frac{1}{4}$ off, and sporting goods prices will be reduced 20%.

   a. Tell how to write a percent as a fraction and as a decimal.

   b. Estimate the sale price of a jacket regularly priced $44. Explain your reasoning.

   c. Tell how to write a fraction as a percent.

   d. Write $\frac{1}{4}$ as a percent. Show your work.

2. The results of one survey are shown in the table.

   a. What is the probability that a person in the community will prefer music? Write your answer as a fraction, a decimal, and a percent.

   b. There are 650 people in the community. Predict how many of them prefer music. Explain how you found your answer.

Activity	People
Contests	9
Amusement Rides	7
Music	6
Exhibits	8

3. You and the committee have designed two spinners for people to win prizes.

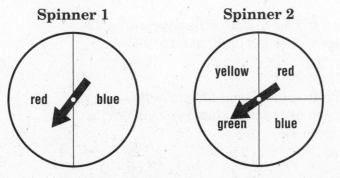

Spinner 1   Spinner 2

   a. In one game, a person spins two spinners. If there is a color match, the person gets a prize. Draw a tree diagram to determine the probability that a person will spin red on the first spinner and red on the second spinner. Explain your answer.

   b. Write a probability problem that can be solved using one of the spinners.

Assessment

7 **Standardized Test Practice**

(Chapters 1–7)

Part 1: Multiple Choice

Instructions: Fill in the appropriate circle for the best answer.

1. Find the rule for the function table. (Lesson 1-6)

Input (x)	
0	2
2	4
5	7

A $x + 1$ **C** $x + 2$

B $x - 1$ **D** $x - 2$

1. Ⓐ Ⓑ Ⓒ Ⓓ

2. The line graph shows Ravi's savings from January through May. What is the *best* prediction for Ravi's July balance? (Lesson 2-3)

F $300

G $350

H $400

J $500

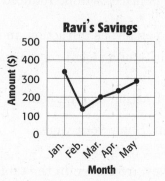

2. Ⓕ Ⓖ Ⓗ Ⓙ

3. **SCHOOL** Thirty students take a math test. The highest score is 97 points, and the range is 29. What is the lowest score? (Lesson 2-7)

A 67   **B** 68   **C** 70   **D** 72

3. Ⓐ Ⓑ Ⓒ Ⓓ

4. Round 1,956.3405 to the nearest thousandth. (Lesson 3-3)

F 2,000   **G** 1,956.340 **H** 1,900   **J** 1,956.341

4. Ⓕ Ⓖ Ⓗ Ⓙ

5. **SHOPPING** Pete buys a CD for $12.39. If he pays with a $20 bill, how much change will he get back? (Lesson 3-5)

A $6.61   **B** $7.59   **C** $7.61   **D** $8.61

5. Ⓐ Ⓑ Ⓒ Ⓓ

6. Twenty out of twenty-five students in Martin's class own a pet. What is the fraction of the class that own pets? Write in simplest form. (Lesson 4-2)

F $\frac{20}{25}$ **G** $\frac{80}{100}$ **H** $\frac{4}{5}$ **J** $\frac{4}{9}$

6. Ⓕ Ⓖ Ⓗ Ⓙ

7. A zoo has two bus tours. The long tour lasts 30 minutes. The short tour lasts 20 minutes. If both buses were at the loading area at 9:00 A.M., when is the first time they will both be at the loading area at the same time again? (Lesson 4-5)

A 9:30 A.M.   **B** 9:50 A.M.   **C** 10:00 A.M.   **D** noon

7. Ⓐ Ⓑ Ⓒ Ⓓ

76

7 Standardized Test Practice *(continued)*
(Chapters 1–7)

8. Find $7\frac{1}{8} - 3\frac{5}{24}$ in simplest form. (Lesson 5-5)

  F $3\frac{11}{12}$ **G** $4\frac{11}{12}$ **H** $3\frac{22}{24}$ **J** $4\frac{1}{4}$ **8.** Ⓕ Ⓖ Ⓗ Ⓙ

9. Eight presidents out of 41 were born in Virginia. Express this as a decimal. (Lesson 7-1)

  A $0.\overline{19512}$ **B** 5.125   **C** $19.\overline{512}$ **D** 51.25   **9.** Ⓐ Ⓑ Ⓒ Ⓓ

10. Five of the first 25 presidents were born in March. What percent of the first 25 presidents were born in March? (Lesson 7-1)

  F 20%   **G** 5%   **H** 25%   **J** 50%   **10.** Ⓕ Ⓖ Ⓗ Ⓙ

11. Write 0.29% as a decimal. (Lesson 7-3)

  A 0.0029   **B** 0.029   **C** 0.29   **D** 2.9   **11.** Ⓐ Ⓑ Ⓒ Ⓓ

12. A number cube is rolled. What is the probability of rolling a prime number? (Lesson 7-4)

  F $\frac{1}{3}$ **G** $\frac{2}{3}$ **H** $\frac{5}{6}$ **J** $\frac{1}{2}$ **12.** Ⓕ Ⓖ Ⓗ Ⓙ

13. In how many ways can you choose 3 pieces of fruit from a bowl of 5 pieces? (Lesson 7-5)

  A 15   **B** 10   **C** 8   **D** 3   **13.** Ⓐ Ⓑ Ⓒ Ⓓ

Part 2: Short Response

Instructions: Write answers to short response in the space provided.

14. What is the least common multiple of 4 and 14? (Lesson 4-5)

  14. _____

15. Owen rolls a number cube 84 times. Predict how many times he rolls a 6. (Lesson 7-6)

  15. _____

Assessment

7 Standardized Test Practice (continued)

(Chapters 1–7)

16. Write 3^3 in words. (Lesson 1-3)

16. _____

17. **ASTRONOMY** Earth revolves once around the sun about every 365.256 days. Round 365.256 to the nearest hundredth. (Lesson 3-3)

17. _____

18. Write $\frac{13}{15}$ as a decimal. (Lesson 4-8)

18. _____

19. **ALGEBRA** Evaluate $c + d$ if $c = \frac{5}{6}$ and $d = \frac{3}{8}$. Write in simplest form. (Lesson 5-5)

19. _____

20. Write the ratio 162 heartbeats in 60 seconds as a unit rate. (Lesson 6-1)

20. _____

21. Write 165% as a fraction in simplest form. (Lesson 7-1)

21. _____

22. One marble is chosen without looking from a bag of 3 red marbles and 27 black marbles. What is P(not black)? (Lesson 7-4)

22. _____

23. **BOOKS** Twelve out of thirty books in Leo's bookcase are mysteries. If ten books are picked at random, about how many will be mysteries? (Lesson 7-6)

23. _____

24. **a.** Identify the percent that is modeled. (Lesson 7-1a)

24a. _____

    b. Write this percent as a fraction in simplest form. Explain each step of your solution. (Lesson 7-1)

24b. _____

    c. Write this percent as a decimal. Explain your solution. (Lesson 7-3)

24c. _____

7 **Unit 3 Test**
(Chapters 6 and 7)

1. Write the ratio *30 shots made out of 45 attempted* as a fraction in simplest form.

1. _____

2. Write the rate *24 batteries in 3 packs* as a unit rate.

2. _____

3. **MONEY** Tanya bought 5 postcards for $2. How much will she spend on 10 postcards?

Number of Postcards	5	10
Money Spent ($)	2	■

3. _____

Determine if the quantities in each pair of ratios or rates are proportional. Explain your reasoning and express each proportional relationship as a proportion.

4. 18 boys to 24 girls; 6 boys to 8 girls

4: _____

5. 5 laps to 25 minutes; 10 laps to 40 minutes

5: _____

Solve each proportion.

6. $\frac{6}{10} = \frac{n}{40}$

6. _____

7. $\frac{5}{9} = \frac{25}{x}$

7. _____

8. $\frac{w}{15} = \frac{33}{45}$

8. _____

Use the table at the below for Questions 9 and 10.

Position	5	6	7	8	n
Value of Term	0	1	2	3	■

9. Use words and symbols to describe the value of each term as a function of its position.

9. _____

10. Find the value of the sixteenth term in the sequence.

10. _____

11. Write 140% as a fraction in simplest form.

11. _____

12. Write 5% as a fraction in simplest form.

12. _____

Assessment

7 **Unit 3 Test** *(continued)*
(Chapters 6 and 7)

13. Write $\frac{4}{5}$ as a percent. 13. _____

14. Write 110% as a decimal. 14. _____

15. Write 0.98 as a percent. 15. _____

16. Estimate 32% of 26. 16. _____

17. Estimate 51% of 129. 17. _____

For Questions 18–21, use the following information.

A set of 15 cards is numbered 1–15. One card is chosen without 18. _____
looking. Find the probability of each event. Write each answer
as a fraction, decimal, and percent. 19. _____

18. $P(5)$ 20. $P(5, 10, \text{or } 15)$ 20. _____

19. $P(\text{less than } 6)$ 21. $P(\text{not } 15)$ 21. _____

22. **WEATHER** There is a 10% chance of rain on Monday. 22. _____
What is the probability it will *not* rain?

23. **FOOD** For breakfast, Billy can have scrambled eggs or fried 23. _____
eggs with hash browns, toast, or a muffin. Draw a tree
diagram to find how many outcomes are possible.

24. **PETS** Amy visits the animal shelter. In how many different 24. _____
ways can she choose 2 cats from the 5 cats up for adoption?

25. **SOCCER** Polly scored 3 goals in her first 15 attempts. Predict 25. _____
how many goals she will score in 25 attempts.

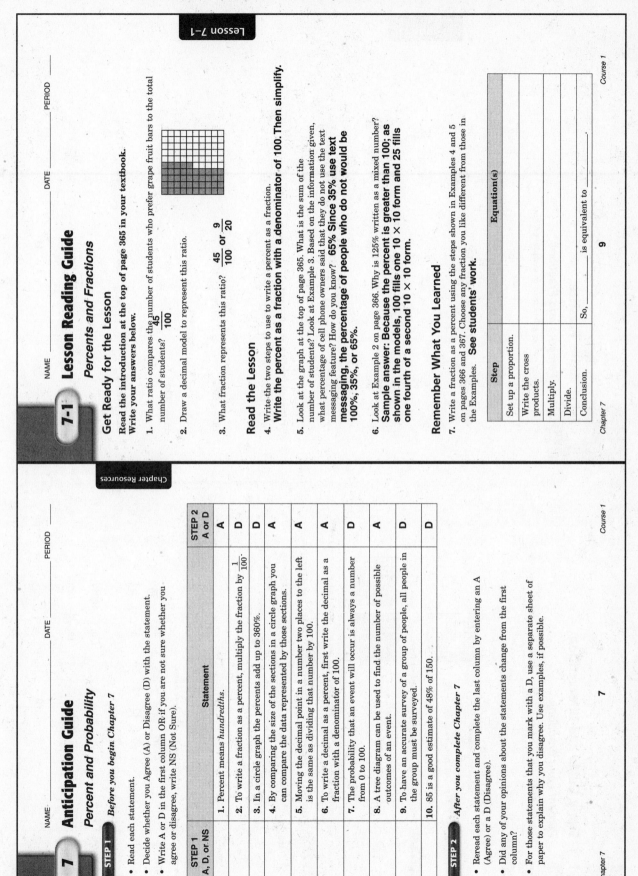

Lesson 7-1

NAME _____ DATE _____ PERIOD _____

7-1 Lesson Reading Guide
Percents and Fractions

Get Ready for the Lesson

Read the introduction at the top of page 365 in your textbook. Write your answers below.

1. What ratio compares the number of students who prefer grape fruit bars to the total number of students? $\frac{45}{100}$

2. Draw a decimal model to represent this ratio.

3. What fraction represents this ratio? $\frac{45}{100}$ or $\frac{9}{20}$

Read the Lesson

4. Write the two steps to use to write a percent as a fraction. **Write the percent as a fraction with a denominator of 100. Then simplify.**

5. Look at the graph at the top of page 365. What is the sum of the number of students? Look at Example 3. Based on the information given, what percentage of cell phone owners said that they do not use the text messaging feature? How do you know? **65% Since 35% use text messaging, the percentage of people who do not would be 100%, 35%, or 65%.**

6. Look at Example 2 on page 366. Why is 125% written as a mixed number? **Sample answer: Because the percent is greater than 100; as shown in the models, 100 fills one 10 × 10 form and 25 fills one fourth of a second 10 × 10 form.**

Remember What You Learned

7. Write a fraction as a percent using the steps shown in Examples 4 and 5 on pages 366 and 367. Choose any fraction you like different from those in the Examples. **See students' work.**

Step	Equation(s)
Set up a proportion.	
Write the cross products.	
Multiply.	
Divide.	
Conclusion.	So, _____ is equivalent to _____.

Chapter 7   **9**   *Course 1*

Chapter Resources

NAME _____ DATE _____ PERIOD _____

7 Anticipation Guide
Percent and Probability

STEP 1 *Before you begin Chapter 7*

- Read each statement.
- Decide whether you Agree (A) or Disagree (D) with the statement.
- Write A or D in the first column OR if you are not sure whether you agree or disagree, write NS (Not Sure).

STEP 1 A, D, or NS	Statement	STEP 2 A or D
	1. Percent means *hundredths*.	A
	2. To write a fraction as a percent, multiply the fraction by $\frac{1}{100}$.	D
	3. In a circle graph the percents add up to 360%.	D
	4. By comparing the size of the sections in a circle graph you can compare the data represented by those sections.	A
	5. Moving the decimal point in a number two places to the left is the same as dividing that number by 100.	A
	6. To write a decimal as a percent, first write the decimal as a fraction with a denominator of 100.	A
	7. The probability that an event will occur is always a number from 0 to 100.	D
	8. A tree diagram can be used to find the number of possible outcomes of an event.	A
	9. To have an accurate survey of a group of people, all people in the group must be surveyed.	D
	10. 85 is a good estimate of 48% of 150.	D

STEP 2 *After you complete Chapter 7*

- Reread each statement and complete the last column by entering an A (Agree) or a D (Disagree).
- Did any of your opinions about the statements change from the first column?
- For those statements that you mark with a D, use a separate sheet of paper to explain why you disagree. Use examples, if possible.

Chapter 7   **7**   *Course 1*

Answers

Answers (Lesson 7-1)

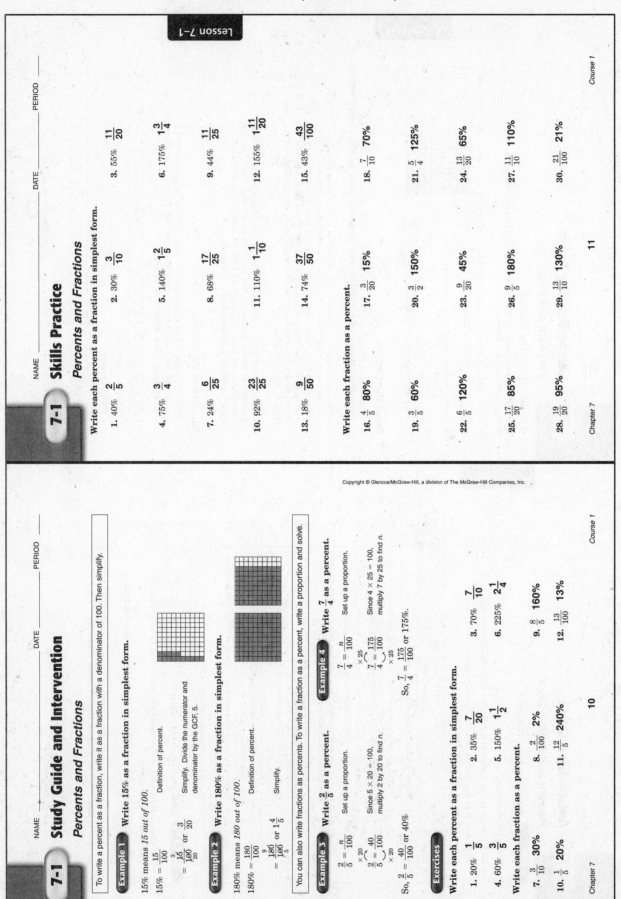

NAME _____ DATE _____ PERIOD _____

7-1 Skills Practice
Percents and Fractions

Write each percent as a fraction in simplest form.

1. 40% $\frac{2}{5}$
2. 30% $\frac{3}{10}$
3. 55% $\frac{11}{20}$
4. 75% $\frac{3}{4}$
5. 140% $1\frac{2}{5}$
6. 175% $1\frac{3}{4}$
7. 24% $\frac{6}{25}$
8. 68% $\frac{17}{25}$
9. 44% $\frac{11}{25}$
10. 92% $\frac{23}{25}$
11. 110% $1\frac{1}{10}$
12. 155% $1\frac{11}{20}$
13. 18% $\frac{9}{50}$
14. 74% $\frac{37}{50}$
15. 43% $\frac{43}{100}$

Write each fraction as a percent.

16. $\frac{4}{5}$ 80%
17. $\frac{3}{20}$ 15%
18. $\frac{7}{10}$ 70%
19. $\frac{3}{5}$ 60%
20. $\frac{3}{2}$ 150%
21. $\frac{5}{4}$ 125%
22. $\frac{6}{5}$ 120%
23. $\frac{9}{20}$ 45%
24. $\frac{13}{20}$ 65%
25. $\frac{17}{20}$ 85%
26. $\frac{9}{5}$ 180%
27. $\frac{11}{10}$ 110%
28. $\frac{19}{20}$ 95%
29. $\frac{13}{10}$ 130%
30. $\frac{21}{100}$ 21%

Chapter 7   11   Course 1

NAME _____ DATE _____ PERIOD _____

7-1 Study Guide and Intervention
Percents and Fractions

To write a percent as a fraction, write it as a fraction with a denominator of 100. Then simplify.

Example 1 Write 15% as a fraction in simplest form.

15% means 15 out of 100.

$15\% = \frac{15}{100}$ Definition of percent.

$= \frac{\overset{3}{\cancel{15}}}{\underset{20}{\cancel{100}}}$ or $\frac{3}{20}$ Simplify. Divide the numerator and denominator by the GCF, 5.

Example 2 Write 180% as a fraction in simplest form.

180% means 180 out of 100.

$180\% = \frac{180}{100}$ Definition of percent.

$= \frac{\overset{9}{\cancel{180}}}{\underset{5}{\cancel{100}}}$ or $1\frac{4}{5}$ Simplify.

You can also write fractions as percents. To write a fraction as a percent, write a proportion and solve.

Example 3 Write $\frac{2}{5}$ as a percent.

$\frac{2}{5} = \frac{n}{100}$ Set up a proportion.

$\frac{2}{5} \overset{\times 20}{=} \frac{40}{100}$ Since 5 × 20 = 100, multiply 2 by 20 to find n.

So, $\frac{2}{5} = \frac{40}{100}$ or 40%.

Example 4 Write $\frac{7}{4}$ as a percent.

$\frac{7}{4} = \frac{n}{100}$ Set up a proportion.

$\frac{7}{4} \overset{\times 25}{=} \frac{175}{100}$ Since 4 × 25 = 100, multiply 7 by 25 to find n.

So, $\frac{7}{4} = \frac{175}{100}$ or 175%.

Exercises

Write each percent as a fraction in simplest form.

1. 20% $\frac{1}{5}$
2. 35% $\frac{7}{20}$
3. 70% $\frac{7}{10}$
4. 60% $\frac{3}{5}$
5. 150% $1\frac{1}{2}$
6. 225% $2\frac{1}{4}$

Write each fraction as a percent.

7. $\frac{3}{10}$ 30%
8. $\frac{2}{100}$ 2%
9. $\frac{8}{5}$ 160%
10. $\frac{1}{5}$ 20%
11. $\frac{12}{5}$ 240%
12. $\frac{13}{100}$ 13%

Chapter 7   10   Course 1

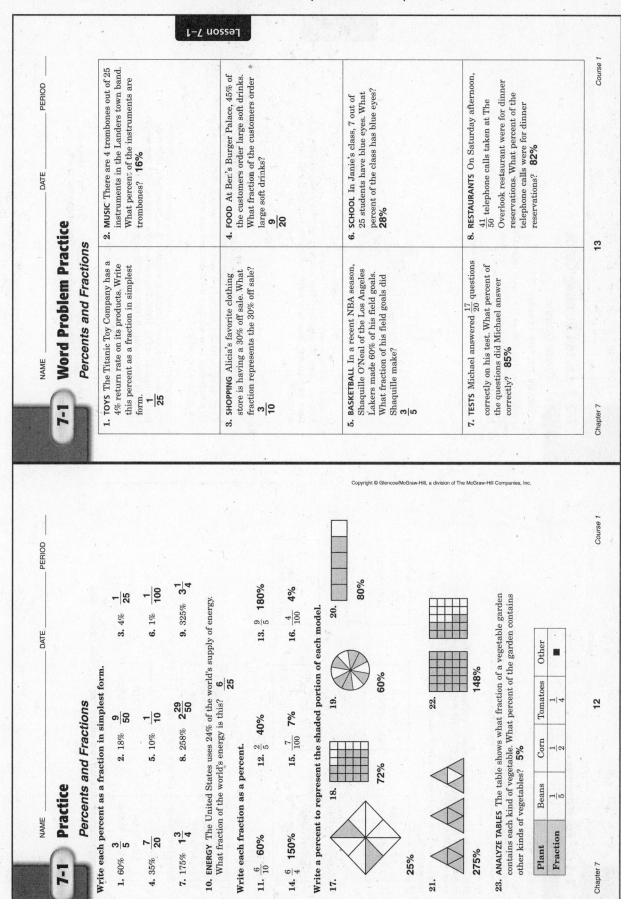

Practice 7-1

NAME _____ DATE _____ PERIOD _____

Percents and Fractions

Write each percent as a fraction in simplest form.

1. 60% $\frac{3}{5}$ 2. 18% $\frac{9}{50}$ 3. 4% $\frac{1}{25}$

4. 35% $\frac{7}{20}$ 5. 10% $\frac{1}{10}$ 6. 1% $\frac{1}{100}$

7. 175% $1\frac{3}{4}$ 8. 258% $2\frac{29}{50}$ 9. 325% $3\frac{1}{4}$

10. **ENERGY** The United States uses 24% of the world's supply of energy. What fraction of the world's energy is this? $\frac{6}{25}$

Write each fraction as a percent.

11. $\frac{6}{10}$ 60%   12. $\frac{2}{5}$ 40%   13. $\frac{9}{5}$ 180%

14. $\frac{6}{4}$ 150%   15. $\frac{7}{100}$ 7%   16. $\frac{4}{100}$ 4%

Write a percent to represent the shaded portion of each model.

17. 25%   18. 72%   19. 60%   20. 80%

21. 275%   22. 148%

23. **ANALYZE TABLES** The table shows what fraction of a vegetable garden contains each kind of vegetable. What percent of the garden contains other kinds of vegetables? 5%

Plant	Beans	Corn	Tomatoes	Other
Fraction	$\frac{1}{5}$	$\frac{1}{2}$	$\frac{1}{4}$	■

Word Problem Practice 7-1

NAME _____ DATE _____ PERIOD _____

Percents and Fractions

1. **TOYS** The Titanic Toy Company has a 4% return rate on its products. Write this percent as a fraction in simplest form. $\frac{1}{25}$

2. **MUSIC** There are 4 trombones out of 25 instruments in the Landers town band. What percent of the instruments are trombones? **16%**

3. **SHOPPING** Alicia's favorite clothing store is having a 30% off sale. What fraction represents the 30% off sale? $\frac{3}{10}$

4. **FOOD** At Ben's Burger Palace, 45% of the customers order large soft drinks. What fraction of the customers order large soft drinks? $\frac{9}{20}$

5. **BASKETBALL** In a recent NBA season, Shaquille O'Neal of the Los Angeles Lakers made 60% of his field goals. What fraction of his field goals did Shaquille make? $\frac{3}{5}$

6. **SCHOOL** In Janie's class, 7 out of 25 students have blue eyes. What percent of the class has blue eyes? **28%**

7. **TESTS** Michael answered $\frac{17}{20}$ questions correctly on his test. What percent of the questions did Michael answer correctly? **85%**

8. **RESTAURANTS** On Saturday afternoon, $\frac{41}{50}$ telephone calls taken at The Overlook restaurant were for dinner reservations. What percent of the telephone calls were for dinner reservations? **82%**

Answers

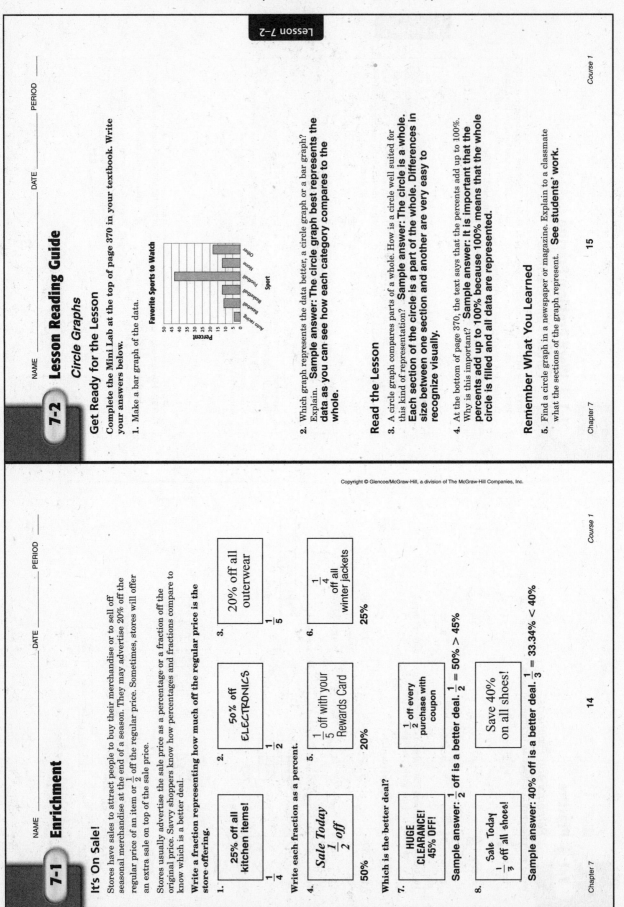

7-1 Enrichment

NAME _____ DATE _____ PERIOD _____

It's On Sale!

Stores have sales to attract people to buy their merchandise or to sell off seasonal merchandise at the end of a season. They may advertise 20% off the regular price of an item or $\frac{1}{2}$ off the regular price. Sometimes, stores will offer an extra sale on top of the sale price.

Stores usually advertise the sale price as a percentage or a fraction off the original price. Savvy shoppers know how percentages and fractions compare to know which is a better deal.

Write a fraction representing how much off the regular price is the store offering.

1. 25% off all kitchen items!
$\frac{1}{4}$

2. 50% off ELECTRONICS
$\frac{1}{2}$

3. 20% off all outerwear
$\frac{1}{5}$

Write each fraction as a percent.

4. Sale Today $\frac{1}{2}$ off
50%

5. $\frac{1}{5}$ off with your Rewards Card
20%

6. $\frac{1}{4}$ off all winter jackets
25%

Which is the better deal?

7. HUGE CLEARANCE! 45% OFF!
Sample answer: $\frac{1}{2}$ off is a better deal. $\frac{1}{2}$ = 50% > 45%

8. Sale Today $\frac{1}{3}$ off all shoes!
Save 40% on all shoes!
Sample answer: 40% off is a better deal. $\frac{1}{3}$ = 33.34% < 40%

Chapter 7   14   *Course 1*

7-2 Lesson Reading Guide

NAME _____ DATE _____ PERIOD _____

Circle Graphs

Lesson 7-2

Get Ready for the Lesson

Complete the Mini Lab at the top of page 370 in your textbook. Write your answers below.

1. Make a bar graph of the data.

Favorite Sports to Watch

Read the Lesson

2. Which graph represents the data better, a circle graph or a bar graph? Explain. **Sample answer: The circle graph best represents the data as you can see how each category compares to the whole.**

3. A circle graph compares parts of a whole. How is a circle well suited for this kind of representation? **Sample answer: The circle is a whole. Each section of the circle is a part of the whole. Differences in size between one section and another are very easy to recognize visually.**

4. At the bottom of page 370, the text says that the percents add up to 100%. Why is this important? **Sample answer: It is important that the percents add up to 100% because 100% means that the whole circle is filled and all data are represented.**

Remember What You Learned

5. Find a circle graph in a newspaper or magazine. Explain to a classmate what the sections of the graph represent. **See students' work.**

Chapter 7   15   *Course 1*

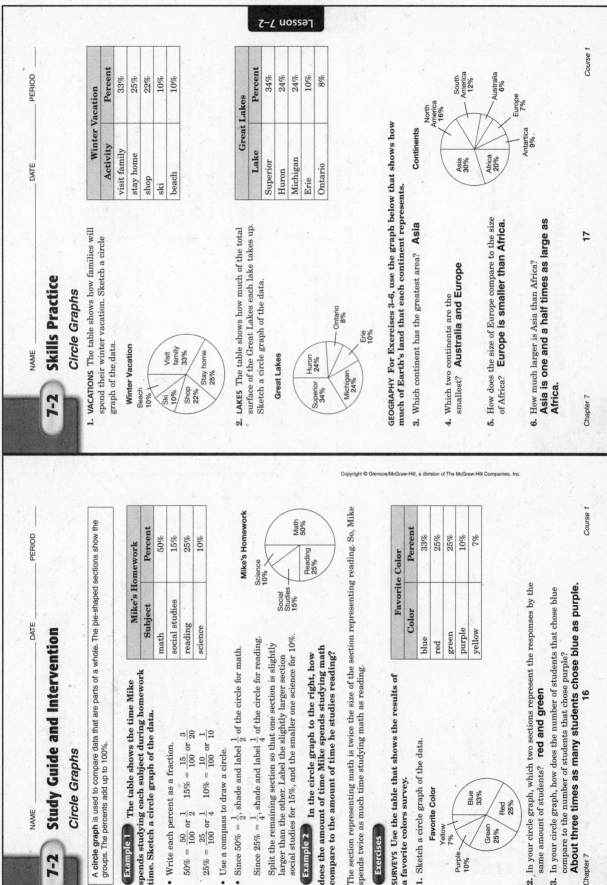

NAME _____ **DATE** _____ **PERIOD** _____

7-2 Study Guide and Intervention
Circle Graphs

A **circle graph** is used to compare data that are parts of a whole. The pie-shaped sections show the groups. The percents add up to 100%.

Example 1 The table shows the time Mike spends studying each subject during homework time. **Sketch a circle graph of the data.**

Mike's Homework	
Subject	Percent
math	50%
social studies	15%
reading	25%
science	10%

- Write each percent as a fraction.

$50\% = \frac{50}{100}$ or $\frac{1}{2}$ $15\% = \frac{15}{100}$ or $\frac{3}{20}$

$25\% = \frac{25}{100}$ or $\frac{1}{4}$ $10\% = \frac{10}{100}$ or $\frac{1}{10}$

- Use a compass to draw a circle.

- Since $50\% = \frac{1}{2}$, shade and label $\frac{1}{2}$ of the circle for math.

Since $25\% = \frac{1}{4}$, shade and label $\frac{1}{4}$ of the circle for reading.

Split the remaining section so that one section is slightly larger than the other. Label the slightly larger section social studies for 15%, and the smaller one science for 10%.

Mike's Homework

Math 50%
Reading 25%
Social Studies 15%
Science 10%

Example 2 In the circle graph to the right, how does the amount of time Mike spends studying math compare to the amount of time he studies reading?

The section representing math is twice the size of the section representing reading. So, Mike spends twice as much time studying math as reading.

Exercises

SURVEYS Use the table that shows the results of a favorite colors survey.

1. Sketch a circle graph of the data.

Favorite Color	
Color	Percent
blue	33%
red	25%
green	25%
purple	10%
yellow	7%

Favorite Color

Blue 33%
Red 25%
Green 25%
Purple 10%
Yellow 7%

2. In your circle graph, which two sections represent the responses by the same amount of students? **red and green**

3. In your circle graph, how does the number of students that chose blue compare to the number of students that chose purple?
About three times as many students chose blue as purple.

NAME _____ **DATE** _____ **PERIOD** _____

7-2 Skills Practice
Circle Graphs

1. **VACATIONS** The table shows how families will spend their winter vacation. Sketch a circle graph of the data.

Winter Vacation	
Activity	Percent
visit family	33%
stay home	25%
shop	22%
ski	10%
beach	10%

Winter Vacation

Visit family 33%
Stay home 25%
Shop 22%
Ski 10%
Beach 10%

2. **LAKES** The table shows how much of the total surface of the Great Lakes each lake takes up. Sketch a circle graph of the data.

Great Lakes	
Lake	Percent
Superior	34%
Huron	24%
Michigan	24%
Erie	10%
Ontario	8%

Great Lakes

Superior 34%
Huron 24%
Michigan 24%
Erie 10%
Ontario 8%

GEOGRAPHY For Exercises 3–6, use the graph below that shows how much of Earth's land that each continent represents.

Continents

North America 16%
South America 12%
Australia 6%
Europe 7%
Antarctica 9%
Africa 20%
Asia 30%

3. Which continent has the greatest area? **Asia**

4. Which two continents are the smallest? **Australia and Europe**

5. How does the size of Europe compare to the size of Africa? **Europe is smaller than Africa.**

6. How much larger is Asia than Africa? **Asia is one and a half times as large as Africa.**

Answers

Answers (Lesson 7-2)

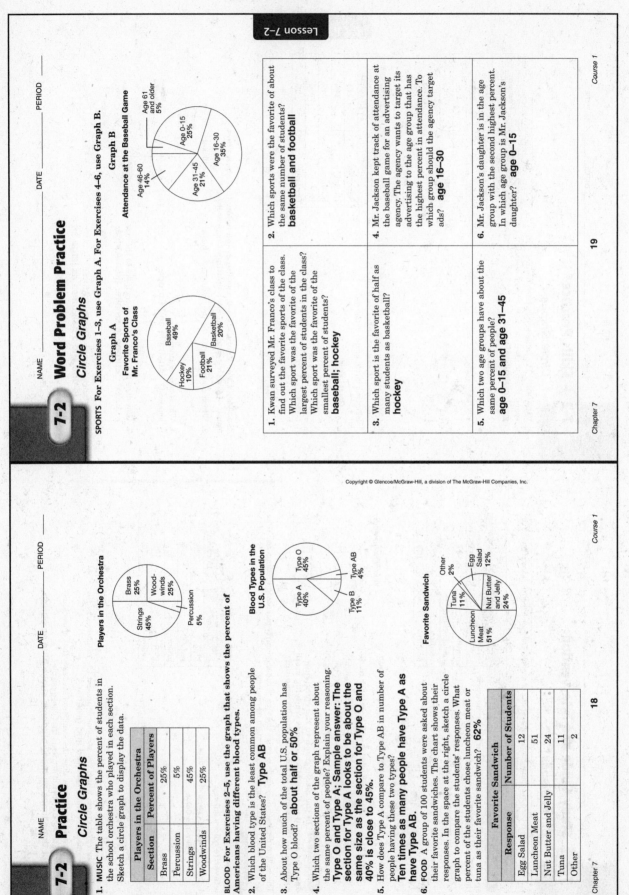

NAME _____ DATE _____ PERIOD _____

7-2 Word Problem Practice
Circle Graphs

SPORTS For Exercises 1–3, use Graph A. For Exercises 4–6, use Graph B.

Graph A
Favorite Sports of Mr. Franco's Class

Baseball 49%
Basketball 20%
Football 21%
Hockey 10%

Graph B
Attendance at the Baseball Game

Age 0–15 25%
Age 16–30 35%
Age 31–45 21%
Age 46–60 14%
Age 61 and older 5%

1. Kwan surveyed Mr. Franco's class to find out the favorite sports of the class. Which sport was the favorite of the largest percent of students in the class? Which sport was the favorite of the smallest percent of students?
baseball; hockey

2. Which sports were the favorite of about the same number of students?
basketball and football

3. Which sport is the favorite of half as many students as basketball?
hockey

4. Mr. Jackson kept track of attendance at the baseball game for an advertising agency. The agency wants to target its advertising to the age group that has the highest percent in attendance. To which age group should the agency target ads? **age 16–30**

5. Which two age groups have about the same percent of people?
age 0–15 and age 31–45

6. Mr. Jackson's daughter is in the age group with the second highest percent. In which age group is Mr. Jackson's daughter? **age 0–15**

19 Course 1

NAME _____ DATE _____ PERIOD _____

7-2 Practice
Circle Graphs

1. **MUSIC** The table shows the percent of students in the school orchestra who played in each section. Sketch a circle graph to display the data.

Players in the Orchestra	
Section	**Percent of Players**
Brass	25%
Percussion	5%
Strings	45%
Woodwinds	25%

Players in the Orchestra

Brass 25%
Woodwinds 25%
Percussion 5%
Strings 45%

BLOOD For Exercises 2–5, use the graph that shows the percent of Americans having different blood types.

Blood Types in the U.S. Population

Type O 45%
Type A 40%
Type B 11%
Type AB 4%

2. Which blood type is the least common among people of the United States? **Type AB**

3. About how much of the total U.S. population has Type O blood? **about half or 50%**

4. Which two sections of the graph represent about the same percent of people? Explain your reasoning.
Type O and Type A; Sample answer: The section for Type A looks to be about the same size as the section for Type O and 40% is close to 45%.

5. How does Type A compare to Type AB in number of people having these two types?
Ten times as many people have Type A as have Type AB.

6. **FOOD** A group of 100 students were asked about their favorite sandwiches. The chart shows their responses. In the space at the right, sketch a circle graph to compare the students' responses. What percent of the students chose luncheon meat or tuna as their favorite sandwich? **62%**

Favorite Sandwich	
Response	**Number of Students**
Egg Salad	12
Luncheon Meat	51
Nut Butter and Jelly	24
Tuna	11
Other	2

Favorite Sandwich

Other 2%
Egg Salad 12%
Tuna 11%
Nut Butter and Jelly 24%
Luncheon Meat 51%

18 Course 1

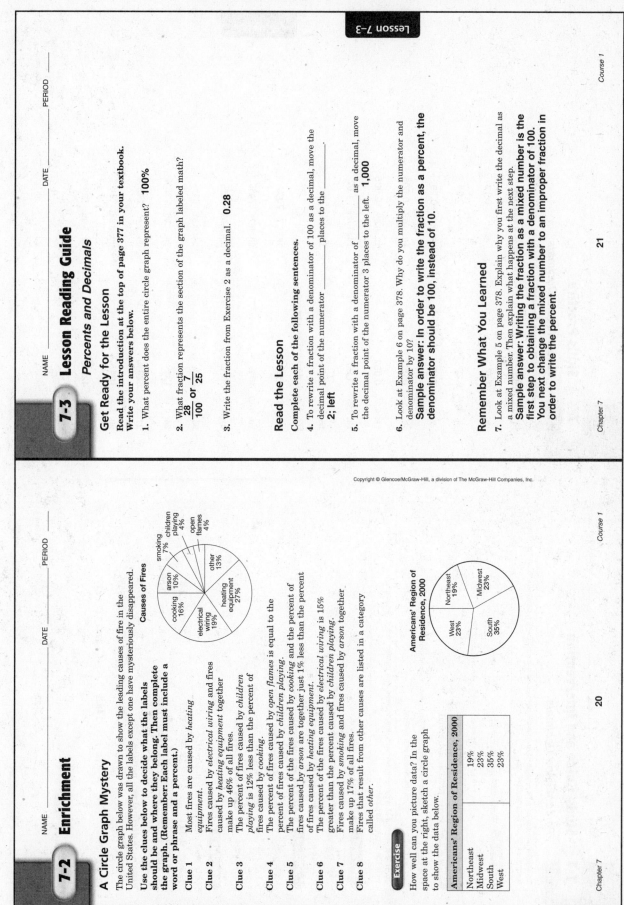

7-3 Lesson Reading Guide

Percents and Decimals

NAME _____ DATE _____ PERIOD _____

Get Ready for the Lesson

Read the introduction at the top of page 377 in your textbook. Write your answers below.

1. What percent does the entire circle graph represent? **100%**

2. What fraction represents the section of the graph labeled math? $\frac{28}{100}$ or $\frac{7}{25}$

3. Write the fraction from Exercise 2 as a decimal. **0.28**

Read the Lesson

Complete each of the following sentences.

4. To rewrite a fraction with a denominator of 100 as a decimal, move the decimal point of the numerator _____ places to the _____. **2; left**

5. To rewrite a fraction with a denominator of _____ as a decimal, move the decimal point of the numerator 3 places to the left. **1,000**

6. Look at Example 6 on page 378. Why do you multiply the numerator and denominator by 10? **Sample answer: In order to write the fraction as a percent, the denominator should be 100, instead of 10.**

Remember What You Learned

7. Look at Example 5 on page 378. Explain why you first write the decimal as a mixed number. Then explain what happens at the next step. **Sample answer: Writing the fraction as a mixed number is the first step to obtaining a fraction with a denominator of 100. You next change the mixed number to an improper fraction in order to write the percent.**

7-2 Enrichment

NAME _____ DATE _____ PERIOD _____

A Circle Graph Mystery

The circle graph below was drawn to show the leading causes of fire in the United States. However, all the labels except one have mysteriously disappeared.

Use the clues below to decide what the labels should be and where they belong. Then complete the graph. (Remember: Each label must include a word or phrase and a percent.)

Clue 1 Most fires are caused by *heating equipment*.

Clue 2 Fires caused by *electrical wiring* and fires caused by *heating equipment* together make up 46% of all fires.

Clue 3 The percent of fires caused by *children playing* is 12% less than the percent of fires caused by *cooking*.

Clue 4 The percent of fires caused by *open flames* is equal to the percent of fires caused by *children playing*.

Clue 5 The percent of the fires caused by *cooking* and the percent of fires caused by *arson* are together just 1% less than the percent of fires caused by *heating equipment*.

Clue 6 The percent of the fires caused by *electrical wiring* is 15% greater than the percent caused by *children playing*.

Clue 7 Fires caused by *smoking* and fires caused by *arson* together make up 17% of all fires.

Clue 8 Fires that result from other causes are listed in a category called *other*.

Causes of Fires

- smoking 7%
- children playing 4%
- open flames 4%
- other 13%
- arson 10%
- cooking 16%
- heating equipment 27%
- electrical wiring 19%

Exercise

How well can you picture data? In the space at the right, sketch a circle graph to show the data below.

Americans' Region of Residence, 2000	
Northeast	19%
Midwest	23%
South	35%
West	23%

Americans' Region of Residence, 2000

- Northeast 19%
- Midwest 23%
- South 35%
- West 23%

Answers

Answers (Lesson 7-3)

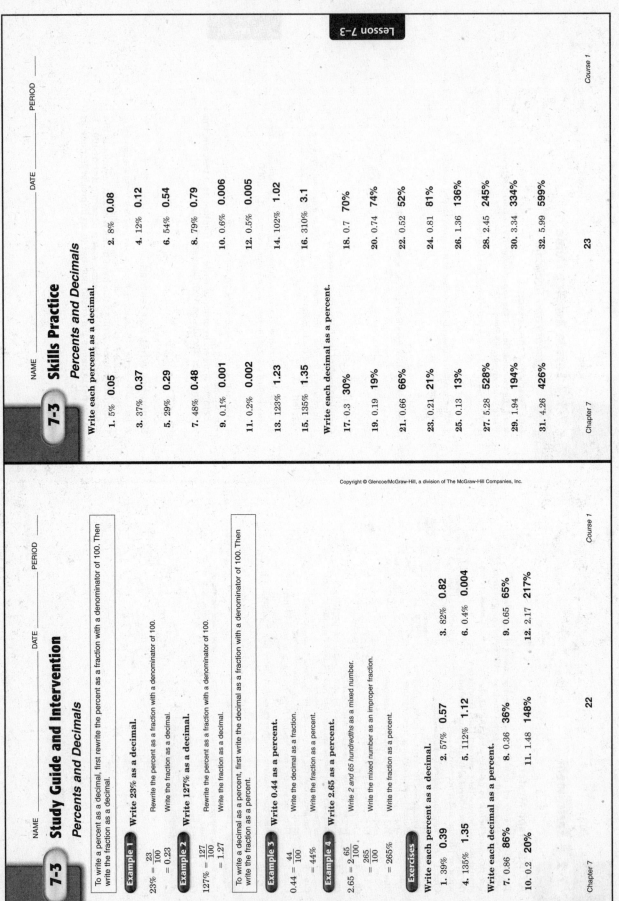

7-3 Skills Practice

Percents and Decimals

Write each percent as a decimal.

1. 5% **0.05**
2. 8% **0.08**
3. 37% **0.37**
4. 12% **0.12**
5. 29% **0.29**
6. 54% **0.54**
7. 48% **0.48**
8. 79% **0.79**
9. 0.1% **0.001**
10. 0.6% **0.006**
11. 0.2% **0.002**
12. 0.5% **0.005**
13. 123% **1.23**
14. 102% **1.02**
15. 135% **1.35**
16. 310% **3.1**

Write each decimal as a percent.

17. 0.3 **30%**
18. 0.7 **70%**
19. 0.19 **19%**
20. 0.74 **74%**
21. 0.66 **66%**
22. 0.52 **52%**
23. 0.21 **21%**
24. 0.81 **81%**
25. 0.13 **13%**
26. 1.36 **136%**
27. 5.28 **528%**
28. 2.45 **245%**
29. 1.94 **194%**
30. 3.34 **334%**
31. 4.26 **426%**
32. 5.99 **599%**

7-3 Study Guide and Intervention

Percents and Decimals

To write a percent as a decimal, first rewrite the percent as a fraction with a denominator of 100. Then write the fraction as a decimal.

Example 1 **Write 23% as a decimal.**

$23\% = \frac{23}{100}$ Rewrite the percent as a fraction with a denominator of 100.

$= 0.23$ Write the fraction as a decimal.

Example 2 **Write 127% as a decimal.**

$127\% = \frac{127}{100}$ Rewrite the percent as a fraction with a denominator of 100.

$= 1.27$ Write the fraction as a decimal.

To write a decimal as a percent, first write the decimal as a fraction with a denominator of 100. Then write the fraction as a percent.

Example 3 **Write 0.44 as a percent.**

$0.44 = \frac{44}{100}$ Write the decimal as a fraction.

$= 44\%$ Write the fraction as a percent.

Example 4 **Write 2.65 as a percent.**

$2.65 = 2\frac{65}{100}$ Write 2 and 65 hundredths as a mixed number.

$= \frac{265}{100}$ Write the mixed number as an improper fraction.

$= 265\%$ Write the fraction as a percent.

Exercises

Write each percent as a decimal.

1. 39% **0.39**
2. 57% **0.57**
3. 82% **0.82**
4. 135% **1.35**
5. 112% **1.12**
6. 0.4% **0.004**

Write each decimal as a percent.

7. 0.86 **86%**
8. 0.36 **36%**
9. 0.65 **65%**
10. 0.2 **20%**
11. 1.48 **148%**
12. 2.17 **217%**

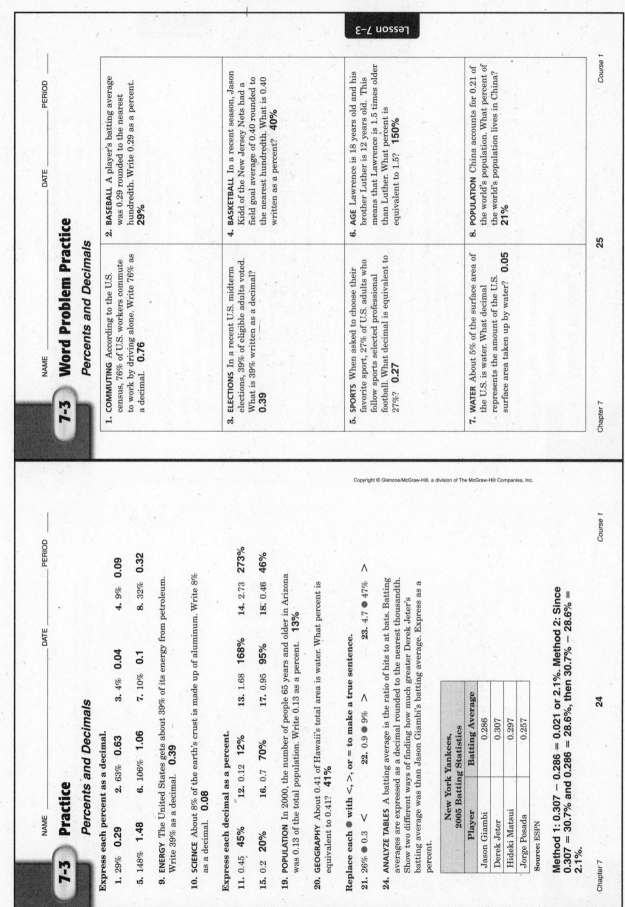

NAME _____ DATE _____ PERIOD _____

7-3 Practice

Percents and Decimals

Express each percent as a decimal.

1. 29% **0.29**   2. 63% **0.63**   3. 4% **0.04**   4. 9% **0.09**

5. 148% **1.48**   6. 106% **1.06**   7. 10% **0.1**   8. 32% **0.32**

9. **ENERGY** The United States gets about 39% of its energy from petroleum. Write 39% as a decimal. **0.39**

10. **SCIENCE** About 8% of the earth's crust is made up of aluminum. Write 8% as a decimal. **0.08**

Express each decimal as a percent.

11. 0.45 **45%**   12. 0.12 **12%**   13. 1.68 **168%**   14. 2.73 **273%**

15. 0.2 **20%**   16. 0.7 **70%**   17. 0.95 **95%**   18. 0.46 **46%**

19. **POPULATION** In 2000, the number of people 65 years and older in Arizona was 0.13 of the total population. Write 0.13 as a percent. **13%**

20. **GEOGRAPHY** About 0.41 of Hawaii's total area is water. What percent is equivalent to 0.41? **41%**

Replace each ● with <, >, or = to make a true sentence.

21. 26% ● 0.3 **<**   22. 0.9 ● 9% **>**   23. 4.7 ● 47% **>**

24. **ANALYZE TABLES** A batting average is the ratio of hits to at bats. Batting averages are expressed as a decimal rounded to the nearest thousandth. Show two different ways of finding how much greater Derek Jeter's batting average was than Jason Giambi's batting average. Express as a percent.

New York Yankees, 2005 Batting Statistics	
Player	Batting Average
Jason Giambi	0.286
Derek Jeter	0.307
Hideki Matsui	0.297
Jorge Posada	0.257

Source: ESPN

Method 1: 0.307 − 0.286 = 0.021 or 2.1%. **Method 2: Since** 0.307 = 30.7% and 0.286 = 28.6%, then 30.7% − 28.6% = 2.1%.

NAME _____ DATE _____ PERIOD _____

7-3 Word Problem Practice

Percents and Decimals

1. **COMMUTING** According to the U.S. census, 76% of U.S. workers commute to work by driving alone. Write 76% as a decimal. **0.76**

2. **BASEBALL** A player's batting average was 0.29 rounded to the nearest hundredth. Write 0.29 as a percent. **29%**

3. **ELECTIONS** In a recent U.S. midterm elections, 39% of eligible adults voted. What is 39% written as a decimal? **0.39**

4. **BASKETBALL** In a recent season, Jason Kidd of the New Jersey Nets had a field goal average of 0.40 rounded to the nearest hundredth. What is 0.40 written as a percent? **40%**

5. **SPORTS** When asked to choose their favorite sport, 27% of U.S. adults who follow sports selected professional football. What decimal is equivalent to 27%? **0.27**

6. **AGE** Lawrence is 18 years old and his brother Luther is 12 years old. This means that Lawrence is 1.5 times older than Luther. What percent is equivalent to 1.5? **150%**

7. **WATER** About 5% of the surface area of the U.S. is water. What decimal represents the amount of the U.S. surface area taken up by water? **0.05**

8. **POPULATION** China accounts for 0.21 of the world's population. What percent of the world's population lives in China? **21%**

Answers

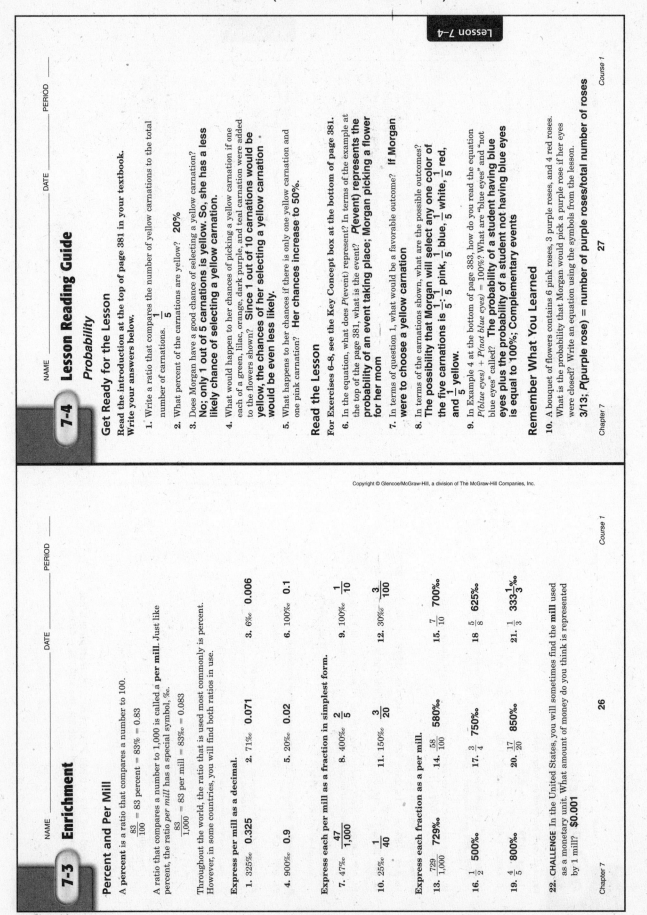

7-4 Lesson Reading Guide

Probability

NAME _____ DATE _____ PERIOD _____

Lesson 7-4

Get Ready for the Lesson

Read the introduction at the top of page 381 in your textbook. Write your answers below.

1. Write a ratio that compares the number of yellow carnations to the total number of carnations. $\frac{1}{5}$

2. What percent of the carnations are yellow? **20%**

3. Does Morgan have a good chance of selecting a yellow carnation? **No; only 1 out of 5 carnations is yellow. So, she has a less likely chance of selecting a yellow carnation.**

4. What would happen to her chances of picking a yellow carnation if one each of a green, lilac, orange, dark purple, and teal carnation were added to the flowers shown? **Since 1 out of 10 carnations would be yellow, the chances of her selecting a yellow carnation would be even less likely.**

5. What happens to her chances if there is only one yellow carnation and one pink carnation? **Her chances increase to 50%.**

Read the Lesson

6. For Exercises 6–8, see the Key Concept box at the bottom of page 381.

6. In the equation, what does *P*(event) represent? In terms of the example at the top of the page 381, what is the event? ***P*(event) represents the probability of an event taking place; Morgan picking a flower for her mom**

7. In terms of question 1, what would be a favorable outcome? **If Morgan were to choose a yellow carnation**

8. In terms of the carnations shown, what are the possible outcomes? **The possibility that Morgan will select any one color of the five carnations is $\frac{1}{5}$: $\frac{1}{5}$ pink, $\frac{1}{5}$ blue, $\frac{1}{5}$ white, $\frac{1}{5}$ red, and $\frac{1}{5}$ yellow.**

9. In Example 4 at the bottom of page 383, how do you read the equation *P*(blue eyes) + *P*(not blue eyes) = 100%? What are "blue eyes" and "not blue eyes" called? **The probability of a student having blue eyes plus the probability of a student not having blue eyes is equal to 100%; Complementary events**

Remember What You Learned

10. A bouquet of flowers contains 6 pink roses, 3 purple roses, and 4 red roses. What is the probability that Morgan would pick a purple rose if her eyes were closed? Write an equation using the symbols from the lesson. **3/13; *P*(purple rose) = number of purple roses/total number of roses**

Chapter 7   27   *Course 1*

7-3 Enrichment

NAME _____ DATE _____ PERIOD _____

Percent and Per Mill

A **percent** is a ratio that compares a number to 100.

$$\frac{83}{100} = 83 \text{ percent} = 83\% = 0.83$$

A ratio that compares a number to 1,000 is called a **per mill**. Just like percent, the ratio *per mill* has a special symbol, ‰.

$$\frac{83}{1,000} = 83 \text{ per mill} = 83‰ = 0.083$$

Throughout the world, the ratio that is used most commonly is percent. However, in some countries, you will find both ratios in use.

Express per mill as a decimal.

1. 325‰ **0.325**   2. 71‰ **0.071**   3. 6‰ **0.006**

4. 900‰ **0.9**   5. 20‰ **0.02**   6. 100‰ **0.1**

Express each per mill as a fraction in simplest form.

7. 47‰ $\frac{47}{1,000}$ 8. 400‰ $\frac{2}{5}$ 9. 100‰ $\frac{1}{10}$

10. 25‰ $\frac{1}{40}$ 11. 150‰ $\frac{3}{20}$ 12. 30‰ $\frac{3}{100}$

Express each fraction as a per mill.

13. $\frac{729}{1,000}$ **729‰**   14. $\frac{58}{100}$ **580‰**   15. $\frac{7}{10}$ **700‰**

16. $\frac{1}{2}$ **500‰**   17. $\frac{3}{4}$ **750‰**   18. $\frac{5}{8}$ **625‰**

19. $\frac{4}{5}$ **800‰**   20. $\frac{17}{20}$ **850‰**   21. $\frac{1}{3}$ **333$\frac{1}{3}$‰**

22. **CHALLENGE** In the United States, you will sometimes find the **mill** used as a monetary unit. What amount of money do you think is represented by 1 mill? **$0.001**

Chapter 7   26   *Course 1*

NAME _____ DATE _____ PERIOD _____

7-4 Skills Practice
Probability

A card is randomly chosen. Find each probability. Write each answer as a fraction, a decimal, and a percent.

A B S
K Q E
O R

1. $P(B)$ $\frac{1}{8}$, 0.125, or 12.5%

2. $P(Q$ or $R)$ $\frac{1}{4}$, 0.25, or 25%

3. $P(\text{vowel})$ $\frac{3}{8}$, 0.375, or 37.5%

4. $P(\text{consonant or vowel})$ $\frac{8}{8}$, 1, or 100%

5. $P(\text{consonant or A})$ $\frac{3}{4}$, 0.75, or 75%

6. $P(T)$ $\frac{0}{8}$, 0.0, or 0%

The spinner shown is spun once. Write a sentence explaining how likely it is for each event to occur.

7. $P(\text{dog})$ Since the probability of spinning a dog or not spinning a dog is 50%, spinning a dog is equally likely to occur.

8. $P(\text{hamster})$ Since the probability of spinning a hamster is 16.6%, spinning a hamster is less likely to occur.

9. $P(\text{dog or cat})$ Since the probability of spinning either a dog or a cat is 83.3%, spinning a dog or cat is likely to occur.

10. $P(\text{bird})$ Since the probability of spinning a bird is 0%, spinning a bird is impossible to occur.

11. $P(\text{mammal})$ Since the probability of spinning a mammal is 100%, spinning a mammal is certain to occur.

12. **WEATHER** The weather reporter says that there is a 12% chance that it will be moderately windy tomorrow. What is the probability that it will not be windy? $\frac{22}{25}$, 0.88, or 88%

13. Will tomorrow be a good day to fly a kite? Explain. No; a 12% chance means that it is unlikely to be windy.

Chapter 7   29   Course 1

NAME _____ DATE _____ PERIOD _____

7-4 Study Guide and Intervention
Probability

When tossing a coin, there are two possible **outcomes**, heads and tails. Suppose you are looking for heads. If the coin lands on heads, this would be a favorable outcome or **simple event**. The chance that some event will happen (in this case, getting heads) is called **probability**. You can use a ratio to find probability. The probability of an event is a number from 0 to 1, including 0 and 1. The closer a probability is to 1, the more likely it is to happen.

impossible to occur	equally likely to occur	certain to occur
0 $\frac{1}{4}$ or 0.25 $\frac{1}{2}$ or 0.50 $\frac{3}{4}$ or 0.75 1		
0% 25% 50% 75% 100%		

Example 1   There are four equally likely outcomes on the spinner. Find the probability of spinning green or blue.

$$P(\text{green or blue}) = \frac{\text{number of favorable outcomes}}{\text{number of possible outcomes}}$$
$$= \frac{2}{4} \text{ or } \frac{1}{2}$$

The probability of landing on green or blue is $\frac{1}{2}$, 0.50, or 50%.

Complementary events are two events in which either one or the other must happen, but both cannot happen at the same time. The sum of the probabilities of complementary events is 1.

Example 2   There is a 25% chance that Sam will win a prize. What is the probability that Sam will not win a prize?

$$P(\text{win}) + P(\text{not win}) = 1$$
$$0.25 + P(\text{not win}) = 1$$
$$\underline{-0.25 \qquad\qquad = -0.25} \quad \text{Replace } P(\text{win}) \text{ with 0.25.}$$
$$P(\text{not win}) = 0.75 \quad \text{Subtract 0.25 from each side.}$$

So, the probability that Sam won't win a prize is 0.75, 75%, or $\frac{3}{4}$.

Exercises

1. There is a 90% chance that it will rain. What is the probability that it will not rain? $\frac{1}{10}$, 0.10, or 10%

One pen is chosen without looking from a bag that has 3 blue pens, 6 red, and 3 green. Find the probability of each event. Write each answer as a fraction, a decimal, and a percent.

2. $P(\text{green})$ $\frac{1}{4}$, 0.25, or 25%

3. $P(\text{blue or red})$ $\frac{3}{4}$, 0.75, or 75%

4. $P(\text{yellow})$ 0, 0.0, or 0%

Chapter 7   28   Course 1

Answers

Answers (Lesson 7-4)

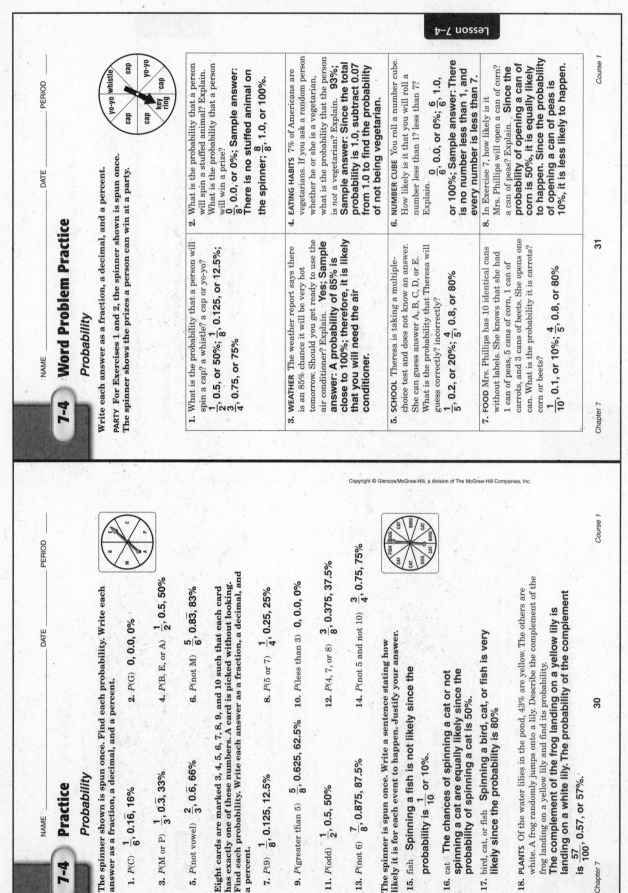

NAME _____ DATE _____ PERIOD _____

7-4 Word Problem Practice
Probability

Write each answer as a fraction, a decimal, and a percent.

PARTY For Exercises 1 and 2, the spinner shown is spun once. The spinner shows the prizes a person can win at a party.

1. What is the probability that a person will spin a cap? a whistle? a cap or yo-yo? $\frac{1}{2}$, 0.5, or 50%; $\frac{1}{8}$, 0.125, or 12.5%; $\frac{3}{4}$, 0.75, or 75%

2. What is the probability that a person will spin a stuffed animal? Explain. What is the probability that a person will win a prize? $\frac{0}{8}$, 0.0, or 0%; Sample answer: There is no stuffed animal on the spinner; $\frac{8}{8}$, 1.0, or 100%.

3. WEATHER The weather report says there is an 85% chance it will be very hot tomorrow. Should you get ready to use the air conditioner? Explain. Yes; Sample answer: A probability of 85% is close to 100%; therefore, it is likely that you will need the air conditioner.

4. EATING HABITS 7% of Americans are vegetarians. If you ask a random person whether he or she is a vegetarian, what is the probability that the person is *not* a vegetarian? Explain. 93%; Sample answer: Since the total probability is 1.0, subtract 0.07 from 1.0 to find the probability of not being vegetarian.

5. SCHOOL Theresa is taking a multiple-choice test and does not know an answer. She can guess answer A, B, C, D, or E. What is the probability that Theresa will guess correctly? incorrectly? $\frac{1}{5}$, 0.2, or 20%; $\frac{4}{5}$, 0.8, or 80%

6. NUMBER CUBE You roll a number cube. How likely is it that you will roll a number less than 1? less than 7? Explain. $\frac{0}{6}$, 0.0, or 0%; $\frac{6}{6}$, 1.0, or 100%; Sample answer: There is no number less than 1, and every number is less than 7.

7. FOOD Mrs. Phillips has 10 identical cans without labels. She knows that she had 1 can of peas, 5 cans of corn, 1 can of carrots, and 3 cans of beets. She opens one can. What is the probability it is carrots? corn or beets? $\frac{1}{10}$, 0.1, or 10%; $\frac{4}{5}$, 0.8, or 80%

8. In Exercise 7, how likely is it that Mrs. Phillips will open a can of corn? a can of peas? Explain. Since the probability of opening a can of corn is 50%, it is equally likely to happen. Since the probability of opening a can of peas is 10%, it is less likely to happen.

Chapter 7   31   Course 1

NAME _____ DATE _____ PERIOD _____

7-4 Practice
Probability

The spinner shown is spun once. Find each probability. Write each answer as a fraction, a decimal, and a percent.

1. $P(C)$ $\frac{1}{6}$, $0.1\overline{6}$, 16%
2. $P(G)$ 0, 0.0, 0%
3. $P(M$ or $P)$ $\frac{1}{3}$, $0.\overline{3}$, 33%
4. $P(B, E,$ or $A)$ $\frac{1}{2}$, 0.5, 50%
5. $P(\text{not vowel})$ $\frac{2}{3}$, $0.\overline{6}$, 66%
6. $P(\text{not } M)$ $\frac{5}{6}$, $0.8\overline{3}$, 83%

Eight cards are marked 3, 4, 5, 6, 7, 8, 9, and 10 such that each card has exactly one of these numbers. A card is picked without looking. Find each probability. Write each answer as a fraction, a decimal, and a percent.

7. $P(9)$ $\frac{1}{8}$, 0.125, 12.5%
8. $P(5$ or $7)$ $\frac{1}{4}$, 0.25, 25%
9. $P(\text{greater than } 5)$ $\frac{5}{8}$, 0.625, 62.5%
10. $P(\text{less than } 3)$ 0, 0.0, 0%
11. $P(\text{odd})$ $\frac{1}{2}$, 0.5, 50%
12. $P(4, 7,$ or $8)$ $\frac{3}{8}$, 0.375, 37.5%
13. $P(\text{not } 6)$ $\frac{7}{8}$, 0.875, 87.5%
14. $P(\text{not 5 and not 10})$ $\frac{3}{4}$, 0.75, 75%

The spinner is spun once. Write a sentence stating how likely it is for each event to happen. Justify your answer.

15. fish Spinning a fish is not likely since the probability is $\frac{1}{10}$ or 10%.

16. cat The chances of spinning a cat or not spinning a cat are equally likely since the probability of spinning a cat is 50%.

17. bird, cat, or fish Spinning a bird, cat, or fish is very likely since the probability is 80%

18. PLANTS Of the water lilies in the pond, 43% are yellow. The others are white. A frog randomly jumps onto a lily. Describe the complement of the frog landing on a yellow lily and find its probability. The complement of the frog landing on a yellow lily is landing on a white lily. The probability of the complement is $\frac{57}{100}$, 0.57, or 57%.

Chapter 7   30   Course 1

7-4 TI-83/84 Plus Activity
Expected and Actual Probability

NAME _____ DATE _____ PERIOD _____

You can use a TI-83/84 Plus graphing calculator to conduct simulations.

Example Suppose you asked 50 people to choose a number from 0 to 9. Find the expected probability of each possible response or outcome.

Possible Outcome	Expected Frequency	Expected Probability	Possible Outcome	Expected Frequency	Expected Probability
0	5	$\frac{1}{10}$	5	5	$\frac{1}{10}$
1	5	$\frac{1}{10}$	6	5	$\frac{1}{10}$
2	5	$\frac{1}{10}$	7	5	$\frac{1}{10}$
3	5	$\frac{1}{10}$	8	5	$\frac{1}{10}$
4	5	$\frac{1}{10}$	9	5	$\frac{1}{10}$

Instead of asking 50 people, you can simulate the data using a graphing calculator.

Enter: MATH ◄ ▲ ▲ ENTER ENTER

The calculator will display a random decimal. Use the individual digits in the number as if they were responses. Record them in a table like the one below. Repeat this process until you have 50 responses. Find the actual frequency by counting the tallies. Find the actual probability by using the actual frequency.

Outcome	Tally	Actual Frequency	Actual Probability
0			
1			

Exercises

1. Use a graphing calculator to conduct this simulation. Complete the table using your random data. Then find the actual probabilities.
Check students' tables for the correct actual probabilities.

2. Compare your data with those of a friend. Why are they not exactly the same?
Since the calculator gives random numbers, no two sets of data will be exactly the same.

Chapter 7   33   Course 1

NAME _____ DATE _____ PERIOD _____

7-4 Enrichment

Working Backward with Probabilities

Suppose that you are given this information about rolling a number cube.

$P(1) = \frac{1}{2}$ $P(3) = \frac{1}{3}$ $P(5) = \frac{1}{6}$

Can you tell what numbers are marked on the faces of the cube? Work backward. Since a cube has six faces, express each probability as a fraction whose denominator is 6.

$P(1) = \frac{3}{6}$ $P(3) = \frac{2}{6}$ $P(5) = \frac{1}{6}$

So, the cube must have three faces marked with the number 1, two faces marked 3, and one face marked 5.

Each set of probabilities is associated with rolling a number cube. What numbers are marked on the faces of each cube?

1. $P(2) = \frac{1}{3}$ 2. $P(1) = \frac{1}{6}$ 3. $P(1 \text{ or } 2) = \frac{5}{6}$

$P(4) = \frac{1}{3}$ $P(4) = \frac{1}{6}$ $P(2 \text{ or } 3) = \frac{2}{3}$

$P(6) = \frac{1}{3}$ $P(6) = \frac{1}{3}$ $P(1, 2, \text{ or } 3) = 1$

$P(\text{factor of } 4) = 1$

2, 2, 4, 4, 6, 6   **1, 2, 2, 2, 2, 4**   **1, 1, 2, 2, 2, 3**

Each set of probabilities is associated with the spinner shown at the right. How many sections of each color are there?

4. $P(\text{red}) = \frac{1}{2}$ **4 red**   5. $P(\text{yellow or purple}) = \frac{5}{8}$ **2 yellow**

$P(\text{blue}) = \frac{1}{4}$ **2 blue** $P(\text{purple or white}) = \frac{3}{4}$ **3 purple**

$P(\text{green}) = \frac{1}{8}$ **1 green** $P(\text{green or blue}) = 0$ **3 white**

$P(\text{black}) = \frac{1}{8}$ **1 black** $P(\text{yellow, purple, or white}) = 1$ **0 green**
                                              0 blue

6. Suppose that you are given this information about pulling a marble out of a bag.

$P(\text{green}) = \frac{1}{4}$ $P(\text{blue}) = \frac{1}{6}$ $P(\text{red}) = \frac{3}{8}$

$P(\text{yellow}) = \frac{1}{24}$ $P(\text{white}) = \frac{1}{24}$ $P(\text{black}) = \frac{1}{8}$

If the bag contains 48 marbles, how many marbles of each color are there?
12 green, 8 blue, 18 red, 2 yellow, 2 white, 6 black

Chapter 7   32   Course 1

Answers

Chapter 7   **A13**   Course 1

Answers (Lesson 7-5)

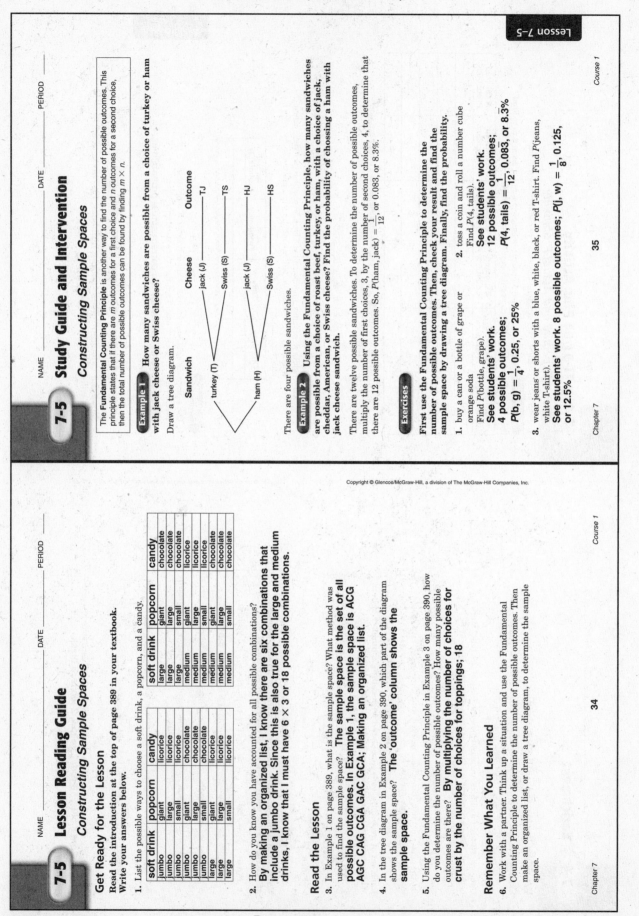

Left Page

NAME _____ DATE _____ PERIOD _____

7-5 Lesson Reading Guide

Constructing Sample Spaces

Get Ready for the Lesson

Read the introduction at the top of page 389 in your textbook.
Write your answers below.

1. List the possible ways to choose a soft drink, a popcorn, and a candy.

soft drink	popcorn	candy	soft drink	popcorn	candy
jumbo	giant	licorice	large	giant	chocolate
jumbo	giant	chocolate	large	large	chocolate
jumbo	small	licorice	large	small	chocolate
jumbo	giant	licorice	medium	giant	licorice
jumbo	large	chocolate	medium	large	licorice
jumbo	small	chocolate	medium	small	licorice
jumbo	giant	licorice	medium	giant	chocolate
large	large	licorice	medium	large	chocolate
large	small	licorice	medium	small	chocolate

2. How do you know you have accounted for all possible combinations?
By making an organized list, I know there are six combinations that
include a jumbo drink. Since this is also true for the large and medium
drinks, I know that I must have 6 × 3 or 18 possible combinations.

Read the Lesson

3. In Example 1 on page 389, what is the sample space? What method was
used to find the sample space? **The sample space is the set of all**
possible outcomes. In Example 1, the sample space is ACG
AGC CAG CGA GAC GCA; Making an organized list.

4. In the tree diagram in Example 2 on page 390, which part of the diagram
shows the sample space? **The 'outcome' column shows the**
sample space.

5. Using the Fundamental Counting Principle in Example 3 on page 390, how
do you determine the number of possible outcomes? How many possible
outcomes are there? **By multiplying the number of choices for**
crust by the number of choices for toppings; 18

Remember What You Learned

6. Work with a partner. Think up a situation and use the Fundamental
Counting Principle to determine the number of possible outcomes. Then
make an organized list, or draw a tree diagram, to determine the sample
space.

Right Page

NAME _____ DATE _____ PERIOD _____

7-5 Study Guide and Intervention

Constructing Sample Spaces

The **Fundamental Counting Principle** is another way to find the number of possible outcomes. This
principle states that if there are m outcomes for a first choice and n outcomes for a second choice,
then the total number of possible outcomes can be found by finding $m \times n$.

Example 1 **How many sandwiches are possible from a choice of turkey or ham**
with jack cheese or Swiss cheese?

Draw a tree diagram.

Sandwich	Cheese	Outcome
turkey (T)	jack (J)	TJ
	Swiss (S)	TS
ham (H)	jack (J)	HJ
	Swiss (S)	HS

There are four possible sandwiches.

Example 2 **Using the Fundamental Counting Principle, how many sandwiches**
are possible from a choice of roast beef, turkey, or ham, with a choice of jack,
cheddar, American, or Swiss cheese? Find the probability of choosing a ham with
jack cheese sandwich.

There are twelve possible sandwiches. To determine the number of possible outcomes,
multiply the number of first choices, 3, by the number of second choices, 4, to determine that
there are 12 possible outcomes. So, $P(\text{ham, jack}) = \frac{1}{12}$, or 0.083, or 8.3%.

Exercises

First use the Fundamental Counting Principle to determine the
number of possible outcomes. Then, check your result and find the
sample space by drawing a tree diagram. Finally, find the probability.

1. buy a can or a bottle of grape or
   orange soda
   Find $P(\text{bottle, grape})$.
   See students' work.
   4 possible outcomes;
   $P(b, g) = \frac{1}{4}$, 0.25, or 25%

2. toss a coin and roll a number cube
   Find $P(4, \text{tails})$.
   See students' work.
   12 possible outcomes;
   $P(4, \text{tails}) = \frac{1}{12}$, $0.08\overline{3}$, or $8.\overline{3}$%

3. wear jeans or shorts with a blue, white, black, or red T-shirt. Find $P(\text{jeans},$
   white T-shirt).
   See students' work. 8 possible outcomes; $P(j, w) = \frac{1}{8}$, 0.125,
   or 12.5%

Answers (Lesson 7-5)

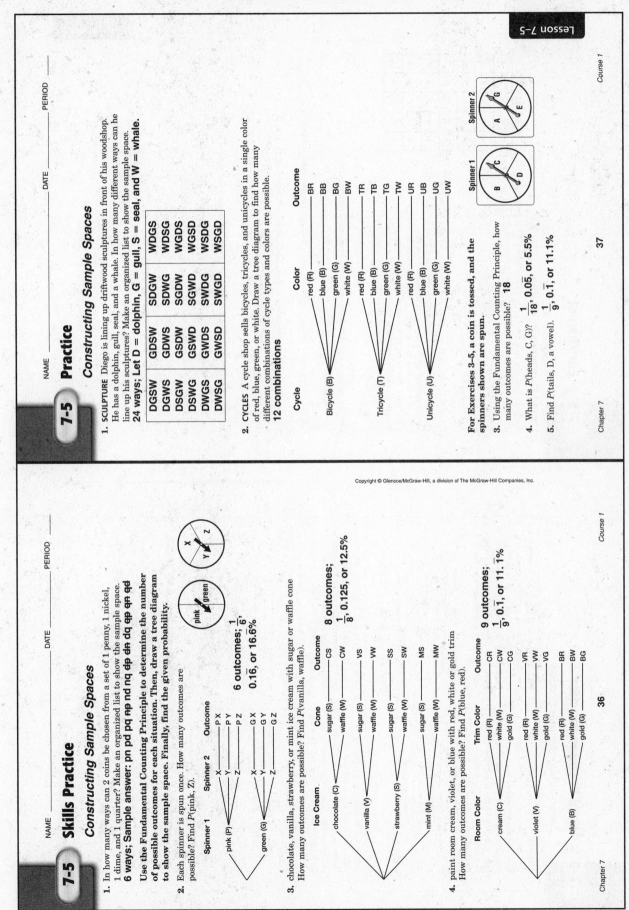

NAME _____ DATE _____ PERIOD _____

7-5 Practice

Constructing Sample Spaces

1. SCULPTURE Diego is lining up driftwood sculptures in front of his woodshop. He has a dolphin, gull, seal, and a whale. In how many different ways can he line up his sculptures? Make an organized list to show the sample space.
24 ways; Let D = dolphin, G = gull, S = seal, and W = whale.

DGSW	GDSW	SDGW	WDGS
DGWS	GDWS	SDWG	WDSG
DSGW	GSDW	SGDW	WGDS
DSWG	GSWD	SGWD	WGSD
DWGS	GWDS	SWDG	WSDG
DWSG	GWSD	SWGD	WSGD

2. CYCLES A cycle shop sells bicycles, tricycles, and unicycles in a single color of red, blue, green, or white. Draw a tree diagram to find how many different combinations of cycle types and colors are possible.
12 combinations

Cycle	Color	Outcome
Bicycle (B)	red (R)	BR
	blue (B)	BB
	green (G)	BG
	white (W)	BW
Tricycle (T)	red (R)	TR
	blue (B)	TB
	green (G)	TG
	white (W)	TW
Unicycle (U)	red (R)	UR
	blue (B)	UB
	green (G)	UG
	white (W)	UW

For Exercises 3–5, a coin is tossed, and the spinners shown are spun.

Spinner 1: B C D
Spinner 2: A G E

3. Using the Fundamental Counting Principle, how many outcomes are possible? **18**

4. What is P(heads, C, G)? $\frac{1}{18}$, $0.0\overline{5}$, or 5.5%

5. Find P(tails, D, a vowel). $\frac{1}{9}$, $0.\overline{1}$, or 11.1%

Chapter 7   37   Course 1

NAME _____ DATE _____ PERIOD _____

7-5 Skills Practice

Constructing Sample Spaces

1. In how many ways can 2 coins be chosen from a set of 1 penny, 1 nickel, 1 dime, and 1 quarter? Make an organized list to show the sample space.
6 ways; Sample answer: pn pd pq nd nq qd

Use the Fundamental Counting Principle to determine the number of possible outcomes for each situation. Then, draw a tree diagram to show the sample space. Finally, find the given probability.

2. Each spinner is spun once. How many outcomes are possible? Find P(pink, Z).

Spinner 1	Spinner 2	Outcome
pink (P)	X	P X
	Y	P Y
	Z	P Z
green (G)	X	G X
	Y	G Y
	Z	G Z

6 outcomes; $\frac{1}{6}$, $0.1\overline{6}$, or 16.6%

3. chocolate, vanilla, strawberry, or mint ice cream with sugar or waffle cone. How many outcomes are possible? Find P(vanilla, waffle).

Ice Cream	Cone	Outcome
chocolate (C)	sugar (S)	CS
	waffle (W)	CW
vanilla (V)	sugar (S)	VS
	waffle (W)	VW
strawberry (S)	sugar (S)	SS
	waffle (W)	SW
mint (M)	sugar (S)	MS
	waffle (W)	MW

8 outcomes; $\frac{1}{8}$, 0.125, or 12.5%

4. paint room cream, violet, or blue with red, white or gold trim. How many outcomes are possible? Find P(blue, red).

Room Color	Trim Color	Outcome
cream (C)	red (R)	CR
	white (W)	CW
	gold (G)	CG
violet (V)	red (R)	VR
	white (W)	VW
	gold (G)	VG
blue (B)	red (R)	BR
	white (W)	BW
	gold (G)	BG

9 outcomes; $\frac{1}{9}$, $0.\overline{1}$, or 11.1%

Chapter 7   36   Course 1

Answers

Answers (Lesson 7-5)

7-5 Enrichment

NAME _____ DATE _____ PERIOD _____

Listing Outcomes in a Table

Suppose that you spin the two spinners below. What is the probability that the sum of the numbers you spin is 5?

	First Spinner			
+	1	2	3	4
1	2	3	4	5
2	3	4	5	6
3	4	5	6	7
4	5	6	7	8
5	6	7	8	9
6	7	8	9	10

Second Spinner

To find this probability, you first need to count the outcomes. One way to do this is to use a table of sums like the one at the right. From the table, it is easy to see that there are 24 outcomes. It is also easy to see that, in 4 of these outcomes, the sum of the numbers is 5. So, the probability that the sum of the numbers is 5 is $\frac{4}{24}$, or $\frac{1}{6}$.

Use the spinners and the table above. Find each probability.

1. $P(\text{sum is 8})$ $\frac{1}{8}$

2. $P(\text{sum is 12})$ **0**

3. $P(\text{sum is greater than 6})$ $\frac{5}{12}$

4. $P(\text{sum is less than or equal to 10})$ **1**

Suppose you roll two number cubes. Each cube is marked with 1, 2, 3, 4, 5, and 6 on its faces. Find each probability. (*Hint:* On a separate sheet of paper, make a chart like the one above.)

5. $P(\text{sum is 9})$ $\frac{1}{9}$

6. $P(\text{sum is 3})$ $\frac{1}{18}$

7. $P(\text{sum is an even number})$ $\frac{1}{2}$

8. $P(\text{sum is a multiple of 3})$ $\frac{1}{3}$

9. $P(\text{sum is a prime number})$ $\frac{5}{12}$

10. $P(\text{sum is a factor of 12})$ $\frac{1}{3}$

11. $P(\text{sum is greater than 12})$ **0**

12. $P(\text{sum is less than 6})$ $\frac{5}{18}$

13. **CHALLENGE** Here is a set of probabilities associated with two spinners. **Answers may vary.**

$P(\text{sum is 4}) = \frac{1}{6}$ $P(\text{sum is 6}) = \frac{1}{3}$

$P(\text{sum is 8}) = \frac{1}{3}$ $P(\text{sum is 10}) = \frac{1}{6}$

In the space at the right, sketch the two spinners.

Chapter 7   39   *Course 1*

7-5 Word Problem Practice

NAME _____ DATE _____ PERIOD _____

Constructing Sample Spaces

1. **OUTINGS** Olivia and Candace are deciding between Italian or Chinese food and then whether to go to a movie, walk in the park, or go for a bike ride. Using the Fundamental Counting Principle, how many choices do they have?

Lunch	Activity	Outcome
Italian (I)	movie (M)	IM
	walk (W)	IW
	bike (B)	IB
Chinese (C)	movie (M)	CM
	walk (W)	CW
	bike (B)	CB

6 choices

2. **PETS** Terence is going to get a parrot. He can choose among a yellow, green, or multi-colored female or male parrot. Draw a tree diagram showing all the ways Terence can choose. What is the probability he will choose a yellow female?

Color	Type	Outcome
yellow (Y)	male (M)	YM
	female (F)	YF
green (G)	male (M)	GM
	female (F)	GF
multi-colored (M)	male (M)	MM
	female (F)	MF

$P(Y, F) = \frac{1}{6}$, $0.1\overline{6}$, or $16.\overline{6}\%$

3. **CAKE** Julia is ordering a birthday cake. She can have a circular or rectangular chocolate or vanilla cake with chocolate, vanilla, or maple frosting. Draw a tree diagram showing all the possible ways Julia can order her cake. How many options does she have?

Shape	Type	Frosting	Outcome
circular (C)	chocolate (C)	chocolate (C)	CCC
		vanilla (V)	CCV
		maple (M)	CCM
	vanilla (V)	chocolate (C)	CVC
		vanilla (V)	CVV
		maple (M)	CVM
rectangular (R)	chocolate (C)	chocolate (C)	RCC
		vanilla (V)	RCV
		maple (M)	RCM
	vanilla (V)	chocolate (C)	RVC
		vanilla (V)	RVV
		maple (M)	RVM

12 options

4. **GAMES** Todd plays a game in which you toss a coin and roll a number cube. Use the Fundamental Counting Principle to determine the number of possible outcomes. What is $P(\text{heads, odd number})$?

Coin	Cube	Outcome
heads (H)	1	H1
	2	H2
	3	H3
	4	H4
	5	H5
	6	H6
tails (T)	1	T1
	2	T2
	3	T3
	4	T4
	5	T5
	6	T6

$P(\text{heads, odd}) = \frac{1}{4}$, 0.25, or 25%

5. **SCHOOL** Melissa can choose two classes. Her choices are wood shop, painting, chorus, and auto shop. List all the ways two classes can be chosen. **WP, WC, WA, PC, PA, CA**

6. **SHOPPING** Kaya has enough allowance to purchase two new baseball caps from the five he likes. How many ways can he choose? **10 ways**

Chapter 7   38   *Course 1*

7-6 Study Guide and Intervention

Making Predictions

A **survey** is a method of collecting information. The group being surveyed is the **population**. To save time and money, part of the group, called a **sample**, is surveyed.

A good sample is:
- selected at **random**, or without preference,
- representative of the population, and
- large enough to provide accurate data.

Examples Every sixth student who walked into the school was asked how he or she got to school.

1 What is the probability that a student at the school rode a bike to school?

$$P(\text{ride bike}) = \frac{\text{number of students that rode a bike}}{\text{number of students surveyed}}$$
$$= \frac{10}{40} \text{ or } \frac{1}{4}$$

So, $P(\text{ride bike}) = \frac{1}{4}$, 0.25, or 25%.

School Transportation	
Method	Students
walk	10
ride bike	10
ride bus	15
get ride	5

2 There are 360 students at the school. Predict how many bike to school.

Write a proportion. Let s = number of students who will ride a bike.

$$\frac{10}{40} = \frac{s}{360}$$

You can solve the proportion to find that of the 360 students, 90 will ride a bike to school.

Exercises

SCHOOL Use the following information and the table shown. Every tenth student entering the school was asked which one of the four subjects was his or her favorite.

Favorite Subject	
Subject	Students
Language Arts	10
Math	10
Science	15
Social Studies	5

1. Find the probability that any student attending school prefers science. **3/8, 0.375, or 37.5%**

2. There are 400 students at the school. Predict how many students would prefer science. **150 students**

Chapter 7   41   Course 1

7-6 Lesson Reading Guide

Making Predictions

Get Ready for the Lesson

Complete the Mini Lab at the top of page 394 in your textbook. Write your answers below.

1. When working in a group, how did your group predict the number of students in your school with green eyes? **By counting the number of students in our group with green eyes, we were surveying a sample of the students in the school. We used what we learned in our group to predict for the school as a whole.**

2. Compare your group's prediction with the class prediction. Which do you think is more accurate and why? **Sample answer: The class prediction is likely more accurate since more students were surveyed.**

Read the Lesson

3. Write the three characteristics of a good sample. **A good sample is selected at random or without preference, representative of the population, and large enough to provide accurate data.**

4. Using the characteristics listed above, do you think that a classroom is a good sample of an entire school? Explain. **Sample answer: It will depend on the information that is being collected. If the information could differ from one classroom to another because of age difference, then it is not a good sample.**

5. If the question of the survey is, "What is your favorite television program?" would you change the sample in any way? If so, how would you change it? **Sample answer: Yes; I would include samples from different classrooms to represent the different age groups, since age probably will influence choice of favorite television programs.**

6. In Examples 1 and 2 on page 395, how is the prediction used? **Sample answer: In Example 1, Lorenzo collects information, creates a ratio, and finds the probability for the event. This probability, if representative of the population, can be used to predict how many members of the total population will respond in the same way (Example 2).**

Remember What You Learned

7. Work with a partner. Find the results of a survey that is of interest to you. For example, to find surveys on favorite TV programs, go to a search engine on the Internet and enter "survey TV programs." Choose one survey. Do you think the survey is a good survey? If so, why? If not, why not and how would you change it? **See students' work.**

Chapter 7   40   Course 1

Answers

7-6 Skills Practice

Making Predictions

Determine whether each sample is a good sample. Explain.

1. 250 people at the beach in the summer are asked to name their favorite vacation spot. **Sample answer: No; people at the beach in summer probably prefer the beach, so they do not represent a larger population.**

2. Every fourth shopper at a grocery store is asked whether or not he or she owns a pet. **Sample answer: Yes; the sample is large enough, random, and represents the community (a larger population).**

For Exercise 3–6, use the table and the following information. A survey of students' favorite sports was taken from a random sample of students in a school. The results are shown in the table.

Students' Favorite Sports	
Soccer	8
Baseball /Softball	3
Volleyball	5
Track & Field	4

3. What is the size of the sample? **20**

4. What is the probability that a student will prefer soccer? $\frac{2}{5}$, 0.4, or 40%

5. What is the probability that a student will prefer volleyball? $\frac{1}{4}$, 0.25, or 25%

6. There are 550 students in the school. Predict how many students at the school prefer track and field. **110 students**

For Exercises 7–10, use the table and the following information. A random sample of 40 flower shop customers was surveyed to find customers' favorite flowers. The table shows the results. The shop expects to sell 50 bunches of flowers on Sunday. How many bunches of each flower should the shop order?

Favorite Flower	
Type	Shoppers
Daisy	8
Gardenia	4
Mum	8
Rose	20

7. daisy **10 bunches**

8. rose **25 bunches**

9. mum **10 bunches**

10. gardenia **5 bunches**

Chapter 7   42   Course 1

7-6 Practice

Making Predictions

QUIZ SHOW For Exercises 1 and 2, use the following information.
On a quiz show, a contestant correctly answered 9 of the last 12 questions.

1. Find the probability of the contestant correctly answering the next question.
$\frac{3}{4}$, 0.75, or 75%

2. Suppose the contestant continues on the show and tries to correctly answer 24 questions. About how many questions would you predict the contestant to correctly answer? **about 18 questions**

CHORES For Exercises 3–6, use the table to predict the number of students out of 528 that would say each of the following was their least favorite chore.

Least Favorite Chore	
Chore	Number of Students
Clean my room	7
Take out the garbage	4
Wash dishes	5
Walk the dog	3
Vacuum or dust	5

3. clean my room **154 students**

4. wash dishes **110 students**

5. walk the dog **66 students**

6. take out the garbage **88 students**

7. **SCIENCE** Refer to the bar graph below. A science museum manager asked some of the visitors at random during a typical day which exhibit they preferred. If there are 630 visitors on a typical day, predict the number of visitors who prefer the magnets exhibit. Compare this to the number of visitors who prefer the weather exhibit.

Visitor Preferences

Electricity 11
Microscope 8
Sound 7
Magnets 12
Weather 7

Number of Visitors: 0 4 8 12 16

About 168 visitors prefer the magnet exhibit, and the number of visitors that prefer the weather exhibit is 98. So, there are about 70 more visitors that prefer the magnets exhibit to the weather exhibit.

Chapter 7   43   Course 1

7-6 Word Problem Practice

Making Predictions

MOVIES For Exercises 1–3, use the table of results of Jeremy's survey of favorite kinds of movies.

Favorite Movie Type	
Type	People
Drama	12
Foreign	3
Comedy	20
Action	15

SLEEP For Exercises 4–7, use the table of results of the Better Sleep Council's survey of Americans to find the most important factors for good sleep.

Most Important Factors for Good Sleep	
Good Mattress	32
Daily Exercise	20
Good Pillows	8
Healthy Diet	11
Other Factors	29

1. **MOVIES** How many people did Jeremy use for his sample? **50 people**

2. If Jeremy were to ask any person to name his or her favorite type of movie, what is the probability that it would be comedy? $\frac{2}{5}$, **0.4, or 40%**

3. If Jeremy were to survey 250 people, how many would you predict would name comedy? **100 people**

4. **SLEEP** Predict how many people out of 400 would say that a good mattress is the most important factor. **128 people**

5. What is the probability that any person chosen at random would not say that a healthy diet is the most important factor? $\frac{89}{100}$, **0.89, or 89%**

6. Suppose 250 people were chosen at random. Predict the number of people that would say good pillows are the most important factor. **20 people**

7. What is the probability that any person chosen at random would say that daily exercise is the most important factor for a good night sleep? $\frac{1}{5}$, **0.2, or 20%**

8. **ICE CREAM** Claudia went to an ice cream shop to conduct a survey. She asked every tenth person who entered the shop to name his or her favorite dessert. Did Claudia select a good sample? Explain. **Sample answer: No, since people in an ice cream shop may be biased toward ice cream as a favorite dessert.**

Chapter 7   44   Course 1

7-6 Enrichment

Odds

People who play games of chance often talk about **odds**. You can find the *odds in favor* of an event by using this formula.

$$\text{odds in favor} = \frac{\text{number of ways an event can occur}}{\text{number of ways the event cannot occur}}$$

With the spinner shown at the right, for example, this is how you would find the odds in favor of the event *prime number*.

There are four prime numbers (2, 3, 5, 7). → 4 = $\frac{2}{3}$
Six numbers are not prime (1, 4, 6, 8, 9, 10). → 6

The odds in favor of the event *prime number* are $\frac{2}{3}$ or 2 to 3.

Suppose that you spin the spinner shown above. Find the odds in favor of each event.

1. number greater than 3 **7 to 3**

2. number less than or equal to 6 **3 to 2**

3. even number **1 to 1**

4. odd number **1 to 1**

5. multiple of 3 **3 to 7**

6. factor of 10 **2 to 3**

To find the *odds against* an event, you use this formula.

$$\text{odds against} = \frac{\text{number of ways an event cannot occur}}{\text{number of ways the event can occur}}$$

Suppose that you roll a number cube with 1, 2, 3, 4, 5, and 6 marked on its faces. Find the odds against each event.

7. number less than 5 **1 to 2**

8. number greater than or equal to 2 **1 to 5**

9. even number **1 to 1**

10. odd number **1 to 1**

11. number divisible by 3 **2 to 1**

12. factor of 12 **1 to 5**

13. **CHALLENGE** The probability of an event is $\frac{2}{3}$. What are the odds in favor of the event? the odds against the event? **2 to 1; 1 to 2**

Chapter 7   45   Course 1

Answers

Answers (Lessons 7-6 and 7-7)

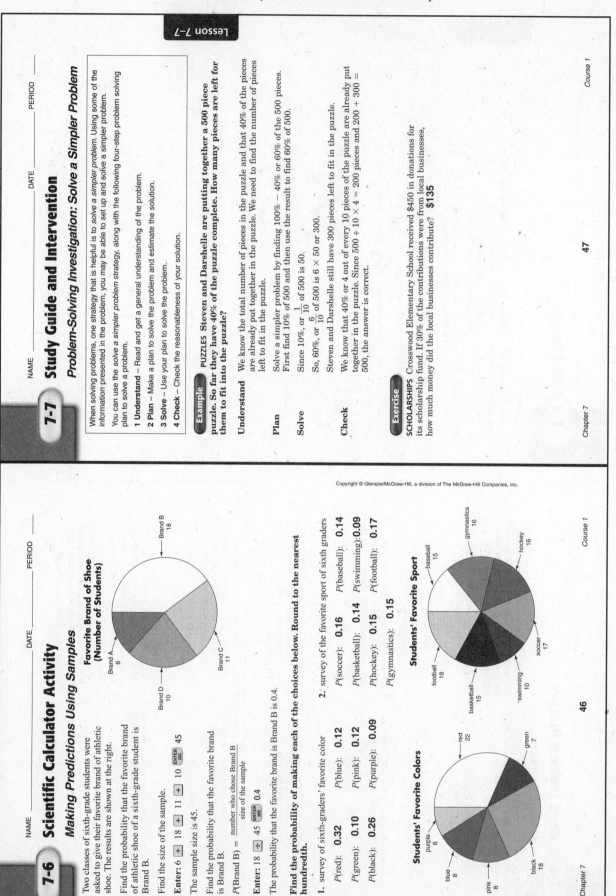

7-7 Study Guide and Intervention

Problem-Solving Investigation: Solve a Simpler Problem

When solving problems, one strategy that is helpful is to *solve a simpler problem*. Using some of the information presented in the problem, you may be able to set up and solve a simpler problem.

You can use the *solve a simpler problem* strategy, along with the following four-step problem solving plan to solve a problem.

1 **Understand** – Read and get a general understanding of the problem.
2 **Plan** – Make a plan to solve the problem and estimate the solution.
3 **Solve** – Use your plan to solve the problem.
4 **Check** – Check the reasonableness of your solution.

Example PUZZLES Steven and Darshelle are putting together a 500 piece puzzle. So far they have 40% of the puzzle complete. How many pieces are left for them to fit into the puzzle?

Understand We know the total number of pieces in the puzzle and that 40% of the pieces are already put together in the puzzle. We need to find the number of pieces left to fit in the puzzle.

Plan Solve a simpler problem by finding 100% − 40% or 60% of the 500 pieces. First find 10% of 500 and then use the result to find 60% of 500.

Solve Since 10%, or $\frac{1}{10}$ of 500 is 50.
So, 60%, or $\frac{6}{10}$ of 500 is 6×50 or 300.
Steven and Darshelle still have 300 pieces left to fit in the puzzle.

Check We know that 40% or 4 out of every 10 pieces of the puzzle are already put together in the puzzle. Since $500 \div 10 \times 4 = 200$ pieces and $200 + 300 = 500$, the answer is correct.

Exercise

SCHOLARSHIPS Crosswood Elementary School received $450 in donations for its scholarship fund. If 30% of the contributions were from local businesses, how much money did the local businesses contribute? **$135**

Chapter 7   47   Course 1

7-6 Scientific Calculator Activity

Making Predictions Using Samples

Two classes of sixth-grade students were asked to give their favorite brand of athletic shoe. The results are shown at the right.

Favorite Brand of Shoe
(Number of Students)

Brand A 6
Brand B 18
Brand C 11
Brand D 10

Find the probability that the favorite brand of athletic shoe of a sixth-grade student is Brand B.

Find the size of the sample.

Enter: 6 + 18 + 11 + 10 ENTER = **45**

The sample size is 45.

Find the probability that the favorite brand is Brand B.

$P(\text{Brand B}) = \dfrac{\text{number who chose Brand B}}{\text{size of the sample}}$

Enter: 18 ÷ 45 ENTER = **0.4**

The probability that the favorite brand is Brand B is 0.4.

Find the probability of making each of the choices below. Round to the nearest hundredth.

1. survey of sixth-graders' favorite color

P(red): **0.32**   P(blue): **0.12**
P(green): **0.10**   P(pink): **0.12**
P(black): **0.26**   P(purple): **0.09**

Students' Favorite Colors

red 22
green 7
black 18
pink 8
blue 8
purple 6

2. survey of the favorite sport of sixth graders

P(soccer): **0.16**   P(baseball): **0.14**
P(basketball): **0.14**   P(swimming): **0.09**
P(hockey): **0.15**   P(football): **0.17**
P(gymnastics): **0.15**

Students' Favorite Sport

baseball 15
gymnastics 16
hockey 16
soccer 17
swimming 10
basketball 15
football 18

Chapter 7   46   Course 1

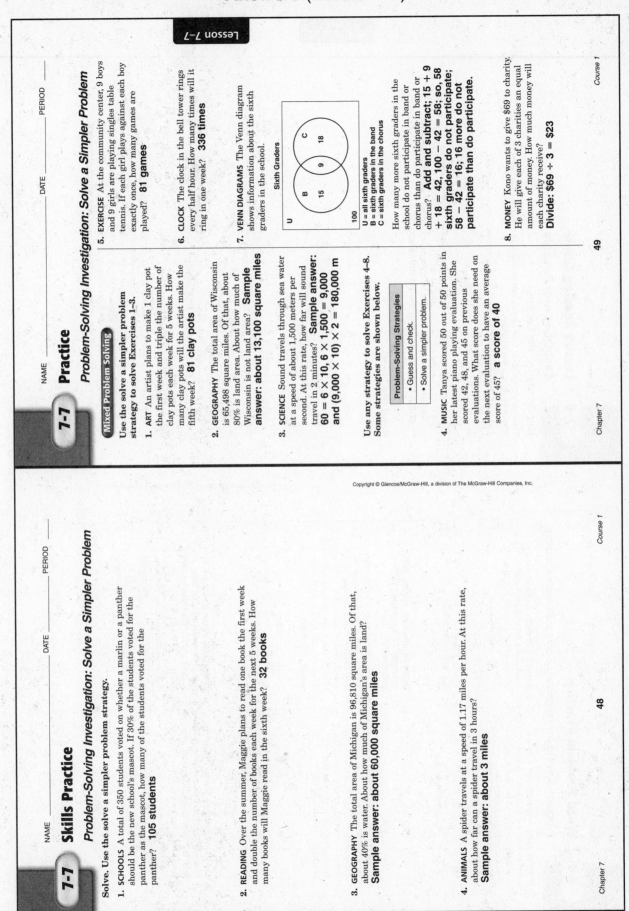

NAME _____ DATE _____ PERIOD _____

7-7 Skills Practice

Problem-Solving Investigation: Solve a Simpler Problem

Solve. Use the solve a simpler problem strategy.

1. **SCHOOLS** A total of 350 students voted on whether a marlin or a panther should be the new school's mascot. If 30% of the students voted for the panther as the mascot, how many of the students voted for the panther? **105 students**

2. **READING** Over the summer, Maggie plans to read one book the first week and double the number of books each week for the next 5 weeks. How many books will Maggie read in the sixth week? **32 books**

3. **GEOGRAPHY** The total area of Michigan is 96,810 square miles. Of that, about 40% is water. About how much of Michigan's area is land? **Sample answer: about 60,000 square miles**

4. **ANIMALS** A spider travels at a speed of 1.17 miles per hour. At this rate, about how far can a spider travel in 3 hours? **Sample answer: about 3 miles**

Chapter 7   48   Course 1

NAME _____ DATE _____ PERIOD _____

7-7 Practice

Problem-Solving Investigation: Solve a Simpler Problem

Mixed Problem Solving

Use the solve a simpler problem strategy to solve Exercises 1–3.

1. **ART** An artist plans to make 1 clay pot the first week and triple the number of clay pots each week for 5 weeks. How many clay pots will the artist make the fifth week? **81 clay pots**

2. **GEOGRAPHY** The total area of Wisconsin is 65,498 square miles. Of that, about 80% is land area. About how much of Wisconsin is not land area? **Sample answer: about 13,100 square miles**

3. **SCIENCE** Sound travels through sea water at a speed of about 1,500 meters per second. At this rate, how far will sound travel in 2 minutes? **Sample answer: 60 = 6 × 10, 6 × 1,500 = 9,000 and (9,000 × 10) × 2 = 180,000 m**

Use any strategy to solve Exercises 4–8. Some strategies are shown below.

Problem-Solving Strategies
• Guess and check.
• Solve a simpler problem.

4. **MUSIC** Tanya scored 50 out of 50 points in her latest piano playing evaluation. She scored 42, 48, and 45 on previous evaluations. What score does she need on the next evaluation to have an average score of 45? **a score of 40**

5. **EXERCISE** At the community center, 9 boys and 9 girls are playing singles table tennis. If each girl plays against each boy exactly once, how many games are played? **81 games**

6. **CLOCK** The clock in the bell tower rings every half hour. How many times will it ring in one week? **336 times**

7. **VENN DIAGRAMS** The Venn diagram shows information about the sixth graders in the school.

Sixth Graders

U = all sixth graders
B = sixth graders in the band
C = sixth graders in the chorus

How many more sixth graders in the school do not participate in band or chorus than do participate in band or chorus? **Add and subtract; 15 + 9 + 18 = 42, 100 − 42 = 58; so, 58 sixth graders do not participate; 58 − 42 = 16; 16 more do not participate than do participate.**

8. **MONEY** Kono wants to give $69 to charity. He will give each of 3 charities an equal amount of money. How much money will each charity receive? **Divide: $69 ÷ 3 = $23**

Chapter 7   49   Course 1

Answers

Answers (Lessons 7-7 and 7-8)

7-8 Lesson Reading Guide

Estimating with Percents

Get Ready for the Lesson

Complete the Mini Lab at the top of page 401 in your textbook. Write your answers below.

Use grid paper to find the fractional portion of each number.

1. $\frac{1}{2}$ of 10 **5**
2. $\frac{1}{5}$ of 10 **2**
3. $\frac{2}{5}$ of 20 **8**
4. $\frac{5}{6}$ of 36 **30**

5. **MAKE A CONJECTURE** How can you find a fractional part of a number without drawing a model on grid paper? **Sample answer: Divide the whole number by the denominator of the fraction, as long as the numerator is 1.**

Read the Lesson

6. Write the fraction for each percent.

$20\% = \frac{1}{5}$	$40\% = \frac{2}{5}$	$60\% = \frac{3}{5}$	$80\% = \frac{4}{5}$
$25\% = \frac{1}{4}$	$50\% = \frac{1}{2}$	$75\% = \frac{3}{4}$	$100\% = 1$
$33\frac{1}{3}\% = \frac{1}{3}$	$66\frac{2}{3}\% = \frac{2}{3}$		

7. Complete the sentence.
When you estimate with percents, you round to numbers that are _____ . **easy to multiply**

Remember What You Learned

8. Work with a partner. Using the fractions and percents in the table you completed for Exercise 6, take turns saying either a fraction or percent. If you say a fraction, your partner writes the corresponding percent. If you say a percent, your partner writes the corresponding fraction. Make sure your partner cannot see the table above. Continue with your practice until you can remember all the fractions and percents. **See students' work.**

7-7 Word Problem Practice

Problem-Solving Investigation: Solve a Simpler Problem

1. **FOOD** Is $8 enough money to buy a dozen eggs for $1.29, one pound of ground beef for $3.99, and a gallon of milk for $2.09? Explain. **Yes; $1 + $4 + $2 = $7 and $0.29 + $0.09 is less than $1.**

2. **SURVEY** The circle graph shows the results of a favorite juice survey. What percents best describe the data?

Favorite Juice

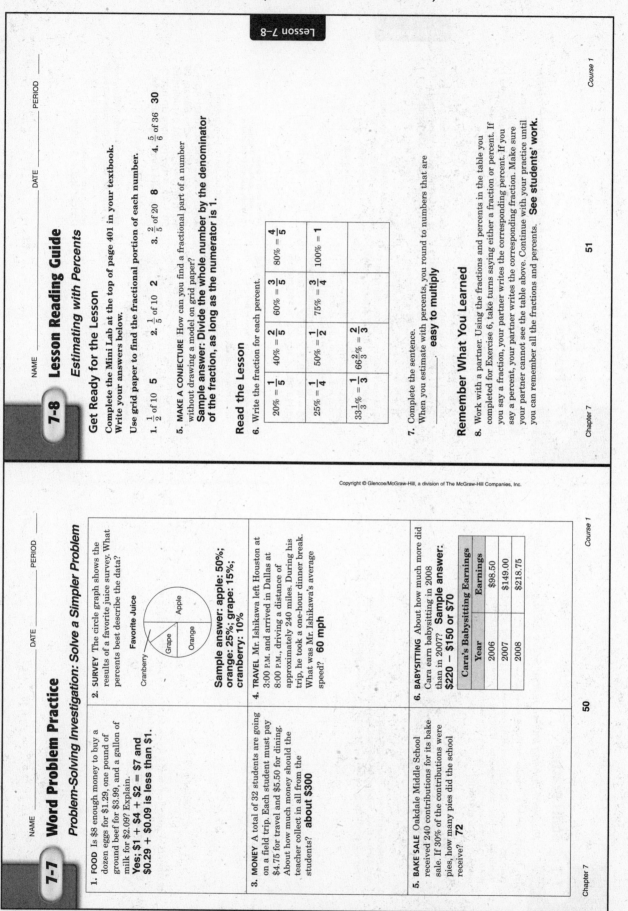

Sample answer: apple: 50%; orange: 25%; grape: 15%; cranberry: 10%

3. **MONEY** A total of 32 students are going on a field trip. Each student must pay $4.75 for travel and $5.50 for dining. About how much money should the teacher collect in all from the students? **about $300**

4. **TRAVEL** Mr. Ishikawa left Houston at 3:00 P.M. and arrived in Dallas at 8:00 P.M., driving a distance of approximately 240 miles. During his trip, he took a one-hour dinner break. What was Mr. Ishikawa's average speed? **60 mph**

5. **BAKE SALE** Oakdale Middle School received 240 contributions for its bake sale. If 30% of the contributions were pies, how many pies did the school receive? **72**

6. **BABYSITTING** About how much more did Cara earn babysitting in 2008 than in 2007? **Sample answer: $220 – $150 or $70**

Cara's Babysitting Earnings	
Year	Earnings
2006	$98.50
2007	$149.00
2008	$218.75

Answers (Lesson 7-8)

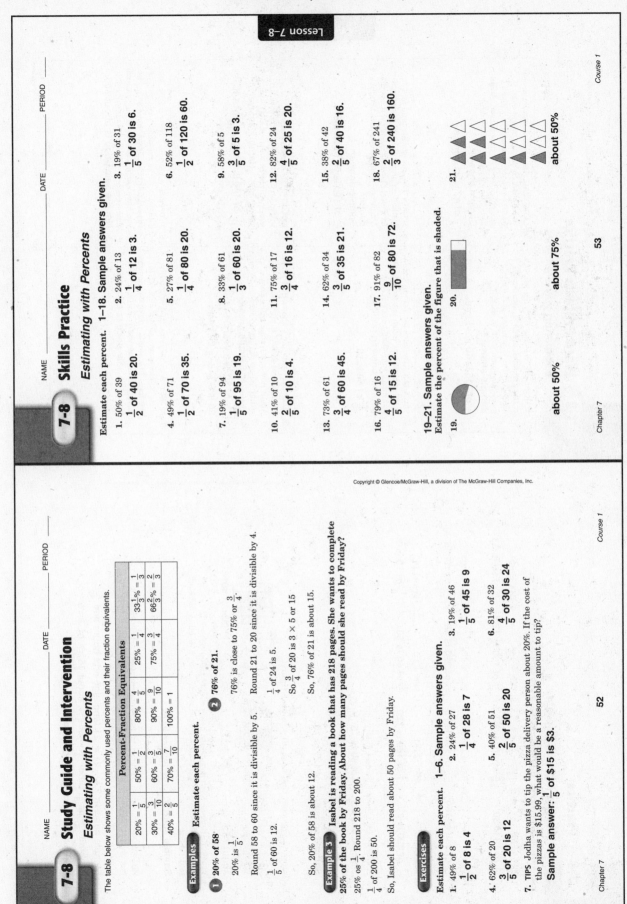

Lesson 7-8

NAME _____ DATE _____ PERIOD _____

7-8 Skills Practice
Estimating with Percents

Estimate each percent. 1–18. Sample answers given.

1. 50% of 39
$\frac{1}{2}$ of 40 is 20.

2. 24% of 13
$\frac{1}{4}$ of 12 is 3.

3. 19% of 31
$\frac{1}{5}$ of 30 is 6.

4. 49% of 71
$\frac{1}{2}$ of 70 is 35.

5. 27% of 81
$\frac{1}{4}$ of 80 is 20.

6. 52% of 118
$\frac{1}{2}$ of 120 is 60.

7. 19% of 94
$\frac{1}{5}$ of 95 is 19.

8. 33% of 61
$\frac{1}{3}$ of 60 is 20.

9. 58% of 5
$\frac{3}{5}$ of 5 is 3.

10. 41% of 10
$\frac{2}{5}$ of 10 is 4.

11. 75% of 17
$\frac{3}{4}$ of 16 is 12.

12. 82% of 24
$\frac{4}{5}$ of 25 is 20.

13. 73% of 61
$\frac{3}{4}$ of 60 is 45.

14. 62% of 34
$\frac{3}{5}$ of 35 is 21.

15. 38% of 42
$\frac{2}{5}$ of 40 is 16.

16. 79% of 16
$\frac{4}{5}$ of 15 is 12.

17. 91% of 82
$\frac{9}{10}$ of 80 is 72.

18. 67% of 241
$\frac{2}{3}$ of 240 is 160.

19–21. Sample answers given.
Estimate the percent of the figure that is shaded.

19. about 50%

20. about 75%

21. about 50%

Chapter 7   53   Course 1

NAME _____ DATE _____ PERIOD _____

7-8 Study Guide and Intervention
Estimating with Percents

The table below shows some commonly used percents and their fraction equivalents.

Percent-Fraction Equivalents				
20% = $\frac{1}{5}$	50% = $\frac{1}{2}$	80% = $\frac{4}{5}$	25% = $\frac{1}{4}$	$33\frac{1}{3}$% = $\frac{1}{3}$
30% = $\frac{3}{10}$	60% = $\frac{3}{5}$	90% = $\frac{9}{10}$	75% = $\frac{3}{4}$	$66\frac{2}{3}$% = $\frac{2}{3}$
40% = $\frac{2}{5}$	70% = $\frac{7}{10}$	100% = 1		

Examples Estimate each percent.

1 20% of 58
20% is $\frac{1}{5}$.
Round 58 to 60 since it is divisible by 5.
$\frac{1}{5}$ of 60 is 12.
So, 20% of 58 is about 12.

2 76% of 21.
76% is close to 75% or $\frac{3}{4}$.
Round 21 to 20 since it is divisible by 4.
$\frac{1}{4}$ of 24 is 5.
So, $\frac{3}{4}$ of 20 is 3 × 5 or 15
So, 76% of 21 is about 15.

Example 3 Isabel is reading a book that has 218 pages. She wants to complete 25% of the book by Friday. About how many pages should she read by Friday?
25% os $\frac{1}{4}$. Round 218 to 200.
$\frac{1}{4}$ of 200 is 50.
So, Isabel should read about 50 pages by Friday.

Exercises
Estimate each percent. 1–6. Sample answers given.

1. 49% of 8
$\frac{1}{2}$ of 8 is 4

2. 24% of 27
$\frac{1}{4}$ of 28 is 7

3. 19% of 46
$\frac{1}{5}$ of 45 is 9

4. 62% of 20
$\frac{3}{5}$ of 20 is 12

5. 40% of 51
$\frac{2}{5}$ of 50 is 20

6. 81% of 32
$\frac{4}{5}$ of 30 is 24

7. TIPS Jodha wants to tip the pizza delivery person about 20%. If the cost of the pizzas is $15.99, what would be a reasonable amount to tip?
Sample answer: $\frac{1}{5}$ of $15 is $3.

Chapter 7   52   Course 1

Answers

Answers (Lesson 7-8)

NAME _____ DATE _____ PERIOD _____

7-8 Word Problem Practice
Estimating with Percents

1. SCHOOL At Westside High School, 24% of the 215 sixth grade students walk to school. About how many of the sixth grade students walk to school?
Sample answer:
$\frac{1}{4}$ of 215 is 50 students.

2. BASKETBALL In a recent regular season the WNBA Houston Comets won 54.76% of their games. They had 42 games in their regular season. About how many games did they win?
Sample answer:
$\frac{1}{2}$ of 42 is 21 games.

3. SALES TAX The sales tax rate in Lacon is 9%. About how much tax would you pay on an item that costs $61?
Sample answer:
$\frac{1}{10}$ of 60 is $6.

4. SPORTS The concession stand at a football game served 178 customers. Of those, about 52% bought a hot dog. About how many customers bought a hot dog?
Sample answer:
$\frac{1}{2}$ of 180 is 90 customers.

5. SLEEP A recent study shows that people spend about 31% of their time asleep. About how much time will a person spend asleep during an average 78 year lifetime? **Sample answer:**
$\frac{1}{10}$ of 80 is 8 years. So, $\frac{3}{10}$ of 80 is 3 × 8 or 24 years

6. BIOLOGY The human body is 72% water, on average. About how much water will be in a person that weighs 138 pounds? **Sample answer:**
$\frac{1}{10}$ of 140 is 14. So, $\frac{7}{10}$ of 140 is 7 × 14 or 98 pounds.

7. MONEY A video game that originally costs $25.99 is on sale for 50% off. If you have $14, would you have enough money to buy the video game?
Yes; the sale price is about $13.

8. SHOPPING A store is having a 20% sale. That means the customer pays 80% of the regular price. If you have $33, will you have enough money to buy an item that regularly sells for $44.99? Explain.
No; the sale price is about $36.

Chapter 7   55   Course 1

NAME _____ DATE _____ PERIOD _____

7-8 Practice
Estimating with Percents

Estimate each percent.   Sample answers are given.

1. 51% of 62
$\frac{1}{2}$ of 60 is 30

2. 39% of 42
$\frac{2}{5}$ of 40 is 16

3. 78% of 148
$\frac{4}{5}$ of 150 is 120

4. 34% of 99
$\frac{1}{3}$ of 99 is 33

5. 74% of 238
$\frac{3}{4}$ of 240 is 180

6. 70% of 103
$\frac{7}{10}$ of 100 is 70

7. 22% of 152
$\frac{1}{5}$ of 150 is 30

8. 91% of 102
$\frac{9}{10}$ of 100 is 90

9. 26% of 322
$\frac{1}{4}$ of 320 is 80

10. 65% of 181
$\frac{2}{3}$ of 180 is 120

11. 98% of 60
$\frac{1}{1}$ of 60 is 60

12. 11% of 10
$\frac{1}{10}$ of 10 is 1

13. Estimate twenty-nine percent of forty-eight.
Sample answer: $\frac{3}{10}$ of 50 is 15

14. Estimate sixty-two percent of one hundred twenty-four.
Sample answer: $\frac{3}{5}$ of 125 is 75

Estimate the percent that is shaded in each figure.

15.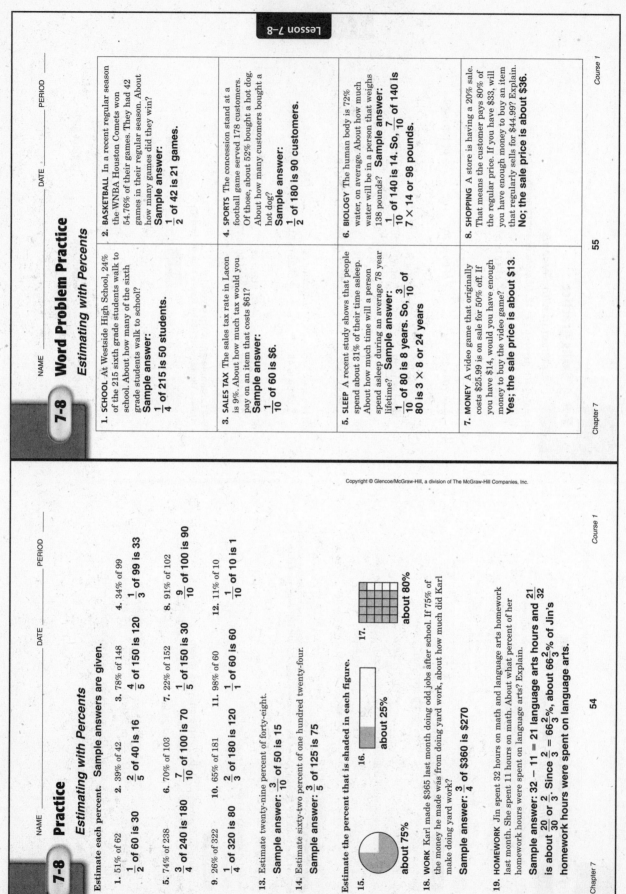
about 75%

16.
about 25%

17.
about 80%

18. **WORK** Karl made $365 last month doing odd jobs after school. If 75% of the money he made was from doing yard work, about how much did Karl make doing yard work?
Sample answer: $\frac{3}{4}$ of $360 is $270

19. **HOMEWORK** Jin spent 32 hours on math and language arts homework last month. She spent 11 hours on math. About what percent of her homework hours were spent on language arts? Explain.
Sample answer: 32 − 11 = 21 language arts hours and $\frac{21}{32}$ is about $\frac{20}{30}$ or $\frac{2}{3}$. Since $\frac{2}{3} = 66\frac{2}{3}\%$, about $66\frac{2}{3}\%$ of Jin's homework hours were spent on language arts.

Chapter 7   54   Course 1

NAME _____ DATE _____ PERIOD _____

7-8 Enrichment

Using 100%, 10%, and 1%

Many people think of 100%, 10%, and 1% as *key percents*.

100% is **the whole.**   100% of 24 = 1 × 24, or 24.

10% is **one tenth** of the whole.   10% of 24 = 0.1 × 24, or 2.4.

1% is **one hundredth** of the whole.   1% of 24 = 0.01 × 24, or 0.24.

Find the percent of each number.

1. 100% of 8,000 **8,000**   2. 10% of 8,000 **800**

3. 1% of 8,000 **80**   4. 10% of 640 **64**

5. 100% of 720 **720**   6. 1% of 290 **2.9**

7. 1% of 50 **0.5**   8. 100% of 33 **33**

9. 10% of 14 **1.4**   10. 100% of 2 **2**

11. 1% of 9 **0.09**   12. 10% of 7 **0.7**

This is how you can use the key percents to make some computations easier.

$$3\% \text{ of } 610 = \frac{?}{}.\qquad 5\% \text{ of } 24 = \frac{?}{}.$$

$$1\% \text{ of } 610 = 6.1,\qquad 10\% \text{ of } 24 = 2.4,$$

so 3% of 610 = 3 × 6.1, or 18.3.   so 5% of 24 = $\frac{1}{2}$ of 2.4, or 1.2.

Find the percent of each number.

13. 2% of 140 **2.8**   14. 8% of 2,100 **168**

15. 4% of 9 **0.36**   16. 20% of 233 **46.6**

17. 70% of 90 **63**   18. 30% of 4,110 **1,233**

19. 5% of 160 **8**   20. 5% of 38 **1.9**

21. 50% of 612 **306**   22. 25% of 168 **42**

23. 2.5% of 320 **8**   24. 2.5% of 28 **0.7**

56

Course 1

Chapter 7

Answers

Chapter 7 Assessment Answer Key

Quiz 1 (Lessons 7-1 and 7-2)
Page 59

1. $\dfrac{1}{20}$

2. $1\dfrac{3}{10}$

3. $\dfrac{2}{5}$

4. 45%

5. 250%

6. 20%

7. math

8. math and gym

Quiz 2 (Lessons 7-3 and 7-4)
Page 59

1. 0.21

2. 0.004

3. 35%

4. 81.2%

5. >

6. <

7. $\dfrac{1}{8}$; 0.125, 12.5%

8. $\dfrac{1}{4}$; 0.25, 25%

9. $\dfrac{3}{8}$; 0.375, 37.5%

10. $\dfrac{7}{8}$; 0.875, 87.5%

Quiz 3 (Lessons 7-5 and 7-6)
Page 60

1. **9 outcomes**

Wig	Shoes	Outcome
red (R)	tennis shoes (T)	RT
	roller skates (R)	RR
	stilts (S)	RS
white (W)	tennis shoes (T)	WT
	roller skates (R)	WR
	stilts (S)	WS
blue (B)	tennis shoes (T)	BT
	roller skates (R)	BR
	stilts (S)	BS

2. **6 outcomes**

Concert	Media	Outcome
1	CD	1, CD
	DVD	1, DVD
2	CD	2, CD
	DVD	2, DVD
3	CD	3, CD
	DVD	3, DVD

3. 62

4. $\dfrac{1}{3}$, $0.\overline{3}$, or $33.\overline{3}\%$

5. 10 goals

Quiz 4 (Lessons 7-7 and 7-8)
Page 60

1. $46

2. 70% × 140 = 98

3. 50% × 80 = 40

4. 25% × 120 = 30

5. C

Mid-Chapter Test
Page 61

1. C

2. G

3. C

4. J

5. D

6. $\dfrac{7}{20}$

7. $1\dfrac{1}{5}$

8. 30%

9. 325%

10. 0.48

11. 0.06

12. 65%

13. 302%

14. $\dfrac{1}{10}$, 0.1, 10%

15. $\dfrac{9}{10}$, 0.9, 90%

Chapter 7 Assessment Answer Key

Vocabulary Test
Page 62

1. _____results_____

2. _____sample_____

3. _____a favorable_____

4. _____an organized_____

5. _____sample space_____

6. _____percent_____

7. _____without_____

8. _____the entire_____

9. ___Complementary___

10. _____survey_____

11. ____sample space____

12. A graph that is used to compare data that are parts of a whole. The data values total 100%.

Form 1
Page 63

1. __D__

2. __H__

3. __A__

4. __G__

5. __C__

6. __G__

7. __B__

8. __H__

9. __D__

10. __G__

11. __C__

12. __H__

Page 64

13. __C__

14. __F__

15. __C__

16. __G__

17. __B__

18. __G__

19. __B__

20. __J__

B: ___37.5%___

Chapter 7 Assessment Answer Key

Form 2A
Page 65

Page 66

1. __C__

2. __F__

3. __A__

4. __G__

5. __B__

6. __F__

7. __B__

8. __H__

9. __C__

10. __G__

11. __C__

12. __H__

13. __B__

14. __H__

15. __B__

16. __H__

17. __B__

18. __H__

19. __C__

20. __F__

B:

blue   yellow

red   yellow

red

1. __D__

2. __J__

3. __B__

4. __G__

5. __A__

6. __J__

7. __A__

8. __G__

9. __B__

10. __H__

(continued on the next page)

Chapter 7 Assessment Answer Key

Form 2B *(continued)*
Page 68

Form 2C
Page 69

Page 70

11. __D__

12. __J__

13. __C__

14. __J__

15. __C__

16. __J__

17. __C__

18. __H__

19. __B__

20. __F__

1. $\dfrac{41}{50}$

2. __80%__

3. __pepperoni__

4. __mushroom and sausage__

5. __About twice as many people like mushroom as like onion as a pizza topping.__

6. __0.06__

7. __4.6%__

8. $\dfrac{4}{15}$, $0.2\overline{6}$, or $26.\overline{6}\%$

9. __68 students__

10. $\dfrac{1}{6}$, $0.1\overline{6}$, or $16.\overline{6}\%$

11. __6 outcomes__

Wire	Bead	Outcome
silver (S)	opal (O)	SO
	jade (J)	SJ
	turquoise (T)	ST
gold (G)	opal (O)	GO
	jade (J)	GJ
	turquoise (T)	GT

12. $\dfrac{1}{10}$, 0.1, or 10%

13. $\dfrac{1}{5}$, 0.2, or 20%

14. $\dfrac{1}{4}$, 0.25, or 25%

15. $\dfrac{19}{20}$, 0.95, or 95%

16. __65%__

17. __10 ways__

18. __10 baskets__

19. Sample answer: $\dfrac{1}{2}$ of 60 is 30

20. Sample answer: $\dfrac{3}{4}$ of 20 is 15

B:

B:

Answers

Chapter 7 Assessment Answer Key

Form 2D
Page 71

1. $\dfrac{3}{25}$

2. 60%

3. dog

4. cow and rabbit

5. About twice as many people chose cats as chose monkeys as a favorite animal.

6. 0.09

7. 93.1%

8. $\dfrac{2}{5}$, 0.4, or 40%

9. 90 students

10. $\dfrac{1}{6}$, 0.1$\overline{6}$, or 16.$\overline{6}$%

Page 72

11. 6 outcomes

Wire	Bead	Outcome
silver (S)	turquoise (T)	ST
	jade (J)	SJ
gold (G)	turquoise (T)	GT
	jade (J)	GJ
bronze (B)	turquoise (T)	BT
	jade (J)	BJ

12. $\dfrac{1}{10}$, 0.1, or 10%

13. $\dfrac{1}{4}$, 0.25, or 25%

14. $\dfrac{19}{20}$, 0.95, or 95%

15. $\dfrac{1}{5}$, 0.2, or 20%

16. 55%

17. 15 ways

18. 15 baskets

19. Sample answer: $\dfrac{2}{5}$ of 250 is 80

20. Sample answer: $\dfrac{1}{2}$ of 250 is 125

B: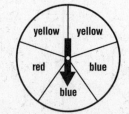

Chapter 7 Assessment Answer Key

1. $0.06; \dfrac{3}{50}$

2. $0.008; \dfrac{1}{125}$

3. $2.3; 2\dfrac{3}{10}$

4. 64%

5. 56%

6. 15%

7. 67%

8. 25%

9. 33%

10. 92%

11. $\dfrac{1}{6}, 0.1\overline{6}$, or $16.\overline{6}\%$

12. $\dfrac{1}{3}, 0.\overline{3}$, or $33.\overline{3}\%$

13. $\dfrac{1}{2}, 0.5$, or 50%

14. $\dfrac{11}{12}, 0.91\overline{6}$, or $91.\overline{6}\%$

15. $\dfrac{12}{12}, 1.0$, or 100%

16. $\dfrac{21}{50}, 0.42$, or 42%

17. 10 ways

18. 5 kernels

19. 9 outcomes

20. $\dfrac{2}{5}, 0.4$, or 40%

21. 252 students

22. $\dfrac{1}{4}, 0.25$, or 25%

23. Sample answer: $\dfrac{3}{10}$ of 20 is 6

24. Sample answer: $\dfrac{3}{4}$ of 120 is 90

25. Sample answer: $\dfrac{1}{10}$ of $40 is $4

B: 5 times

Answers

Chapter 7 Assessment Answer Key

Page 75, Extended-Response Test
Scoring Rubric

Level	Specific Criteria
4	The student demonstrates a **thorough understanding** of the mathematics concepts and/or procedures embodied in the task. The student has responded correctly to the task, used mathematically sound procedures, and provided clear and complete explanations and interpretations. The response may contain minor flaws that do not detract from the demonstration of a thorough understanding.
3	The student demonstrates an **understanding** of the mathematics concepts and/or procedures embodied in the task. The student's response to the task is essentially correct with the mathematical procedures used and the explanations and interpretations provided demonstrating an essential but less than thorough understanding. The response may contain minor errors that reflect inattentive execution of the mathematical procedures or indications of some misunderstanding of the underlying mathematics concepts and/or procedures.
2	The student has demonstrated only a **partial understanding** of the mathematics concepts and/or procedures embodied in the task. Although the student may have used the correct approach to obtaining a solution or may have provided a correct solution, the student's work lacks an essential understanding of the underlying mathematical concepts. The response contains errors related to misunderstanding important aspects of the task, misuse of mathematical procedures, or faulty interpretations of results.
1	The student has demonstrated a **very limited understanding** of the mathematics concepts and/or procedures embodied in the task. The student's response to the task is incomplete and exhibits many flaws. Although the student has addressed some of the conditions of the task, the student reached an inadequate conclusion and/or provided reasoning that was faulty or incomplete. The response exhibits many errors or may be incomplete.
0	The student has provided a **completely incorrect** solution or uninterpretable response, or no response at all.

Chapter 7 Assessment Answer Key

Page 75, Extended-Response Test
Sample Answers

In addition to the scoring rubric found on page A32, the following sample answers may be used as guidance in evaluating open-ended assessment items.

1. a. To write a percent as a fraction, write it with a denominator of 100 and simplify.
To write a percent as a decimal, rewite the percent as a fraction with a denominator of 100. Then write the fraction as a decimal, or move the decimal point two places to the left.

   b. 30% is about $\frac{1}{3}$, $44 is about 45,
   $\frac{1}{3}$ of 45 is 15, $44 - 15 = 29
   The sale price of the jacket is about $29.

   c. To write a fraction as a percent, write a proportion with a fraction equal to $\frac{n}{100}$. Then solve for n and write as $n\%$.

   d. $\overset{\times 40}{\overset{\frown}{\frac{1}{4}}} = \frac{25}{100}$; so $\frac{1}{4} = \frac{25}{100}$ or 25%.
   $\underset{\times 40}{\underset{\smile}{}}$

2. a. $P(\text{music}) = \frac{1}{5}$, 0.2, or 20%

   b. Out of 650 people, 130 will prefer music. Since we know that $\frac{1}{5}$ of the sample preferred music, we set can up a proportion $\frac{1}{5} = \frac{x}{650}$ and solve for x.

3. a.

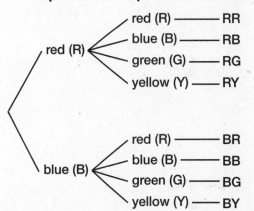

Spinner 1	Spinner 2	Outcome
red (R)	red (R)	RR
	blue (B)	RB
	green (G)	RG
	yellow (Y)	RY
blue (B)	red (R)	BR
	blue (B)	BB
	green (G)	BG
	yellow (Y)	BY

$P(\text{red, red}) = \frac{1}{8}$. There are 8 possible outcomes. Only one outcome has red and red, so 1 out of 8 is the probability.

   b. Sample answer: Find the probability of spinning red or green on Spinner 2.

   $P(\text{red or green}) = \frac{1}{4} + \frac{1}{4}$ or $\frac{1}{2}$.

Answers

Chapter 7 Assessment Answer Key

Standardized Test Practice

Page 76

1. Ⓐ Ⓑ ● Ⓓ

2. Ⓕ Ⓖ ● Ⓙ

3. Ⓐ ● Ⓒ Ⓓ

4. Ⓕ Ⓖ Ⓗ ●

5. Ⓐ Ⓑ ● Ⓓ

6. Ⓕ Ⓖ ● Ⓙ

7. Ⓐ Ⓑ ● Ⓓ

Page 77

8. ● Ⓖ Ⓗ Ⓙ

9. ● Ⓑ Ⓒ Ⓓ

10. ● Ⓖ Ⓗ Ⓙ

11. ● Ⓑ Ⓒ Ⓓ

12. Ⓕ Ⓖ Ⓗ ●

13. Ⓐ ● Ⓒ Ⓓ

14. _____28_____

15. _____14_____

(continued on the next page)

Standardized Test Practice *(continued)*
Page 78

16. ___three cubed___

17. ___365.26___

18. ___$0.8\overline{6}$___

19. ___$1\frac{5}{24}$___

20. ___$\dfrac{2.7 \text{ heartbeats}}{1 \text{ sec}}$___

21. ___$1\frac{13}{20}$___

22. ___$\frac{1}{10}$, 0.1, or 10%___

23. ___4___

24a. ___64%___

24b. ___$\frac{16}{25}$; 64% = $\frac{64}{100} = \frac{16}{25}$___

24c. ___0.64; 64% = $\frac{64}{100} = 0.64$___

Answers

Chapter 7 Assessment Answer Key

Unit 3 Test
Page 79

1. $\dfrac{2}{3}$

2. $\dfrac{8\text{ batteries}}{1\text{ pack}}$

3. $4

4: **Yes; the unit rates are the same,** $\dfrac{18\text{ boys}}{24\text{ girls}} = \dfrac{6\text{ boys}}{8\text{ girls}}$

5: **No; the unit rates are not the same.**

6. 24

7. 45

8. 11

9. **subtract 5 from the position number;** $n - 5$

10. 11

11. $1\dfrac{2}{5}$

12. $\dfrac{1}{20}$

Page 80

13. 80%

14. 1.10

15. 98%

16. **Sample answer:** $\dfrac{1}{3} \times 27 = 9$

17. **Sample answer:** $\dfrac{1}{2} \times 130 = 65$

18. $\dfrac{1}{15}$, $0.0\overline{6}$, or $6.\overline{6}\%$

19. $\dfrac{1}{5}$, 0.2, or 20%

20. $\dfrac{1}{3}$ $0.\overline{3}$, or $33.\overline{3}\%$

21. $\dfrac{14}{15}$, $0.9\overline{3}$, or $93.\overline{3}\%$

22. $\dfrac{9}{10}$, 0.9, or 90%

23. 6

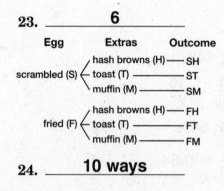

Egg	Extras	Outcome
scrambled (S)	hash browns (H)	SH
	toast (T)	ST
	muffin (M)	SM
fried (F)	hash browns (H)	FH
	toast (T)	FT
	muffin (M)	FM

24. **10 ways**

25. **5 goals**